And God Changed His Mind

Brother Andrew
with
Susan DeVore Williams

Chosen Books

A Division of Baker Book House Co
Grand Rapids, Michigan 49516

© 1990, 1999 by Brother Andrew

Published by Chosen Books
a division of Baker Book House Company
P.O. Box 6287, Grand Rapids, MI 49516-6287

New paperback edition published 1999

Second printing, October 1999

Printed in the United States of America

Library of Congress Cataloging-in-Publication Data

Andrew, Brother.
    And God changed his mind / Brother Andrew with Susan DeVore
Williams.—New pbk. ed.
      p.   cm.
    ISBN 0-8007-9272-6 (paper)
    1. Prayer—Christianity. 2. God—Immutability. I. Williams, Susan DeVore.
II. Title.
BV220.A45   1999
248.3'2—dc21   99-30464

Contents

Foreword

God is not a man, that he should lie. He is not a human, that he should change his mind.

Numbers 23:19 NLT

I said: It is my fault that the right hand of the Most High has changed.

Psalm 77:11 *Khetubim,*
Hebrew Bible

Then the Lord turned from the evil which He had thought to do to His people.

Exodus 32:14 AMP

Is there any sense in praying? If so, is there a prayer big enough to bring about radical change in our world? Or is there a prayer that will change *me,* so God can then use me to do something about the problem? Is there a possibility that He will say, in answer to one of my requests, "How about answering your own prayer?"

This would not be a rebuff, mind you, but a result of God's having noted growth in my spiritual maturity (as a direct outgrowth of my prayers!) so that He now judges me capable of getting involved.

Yes, prayer can and does change the world—but above all, it changes me!

Since I first wrote this book, my own prayer life, not surprisingly, has changed in many ways. So has my preaching and teaching on the subject of prayer. If only I had known some of these things earlier! But we are disciples and learners all the time, are we not?

In recent years I have learned that the most challenging aspect of prayer—real intercessory prayer, that is—is being able to love with sacrificial compassion those for whom we pray. And where else can we learn that but on our knees?

The clearest illustration of this kind of prayer is found in Exodus 32, where Moses and his people are in a situation that reminds me of the world today. Here we see that God's own people, directly defying His express command, have forsaken Him and turned to idolatry, forcing their priest to construct a golden calf.

Understandably God is very angry because they have thwarted His ultimate plan and purpose for Israel—to prepare the way for the coming of their King. Basically, through their disobedience, God's people have destroyed His best-laid plans for all mankind. God is angry to the point where He says to Moses, "Now leave me alone so my anger can blaze against them and destroy them all" (verse 10, NLT). In this passage it is obvious that God is finished with Israel. He is washing His hands of the people in whom He has invested so much.

Often when I look at the world, I think this is how God must feel today, after all the opportunities He has given us: After the massive Bible and tract distributions we have done; after the revivals that have taken place on every continent; after the churches and schools and missions we have built; after the Christian books, magazines, radio and television stations that have spread the Word around the globe; after all the claims by some overzealous Christians that Jesus can return tomorrow because we have finished the job of world evangelization; after all the superficial calculations that we now have more Christians per square inch than ever before in the world—what can the honest Christian do but sit back and say, "What a mess we have made of this world!"

Is God angry with all of this? Yes, He surely is.

But as we continue reading this passage in Exodus, we find something unexpected: Even as God declares His intention to destroy Israel, He holds out a carrot to Moses: "I will make you, Moses, into a great nation instead of them" (Exodus 32:10, NLT).

No man in history ever had that kind of offer! Would any honest, robust, radical Christian standing before God today, I wonder, be able to turn down such an offer? "God, You want to create a new people through *me*—people who will do Your will, keep Your commandments and ultimately reach the world for Christ?"

Amazingly Moses does not seize the honor God has offered him. Instead he pleads with Him: "O Lord! Why are you so angry with your own people? . . . Turn away from your fierce anger. Change your mind about this terrible disaster you are planning against your people!" (verses 11–12, NLT).

Yes, Moses intercedes for his people, and here comes the crunch: In the Hebrew Bible, verse 11 says, literally, that "Moses smoothed the wrinkles in Jehovah's face."

Unless you have access to a Hebrew lexicon, you will not be able to find this phrase, but I advise anyone with a theological background and access to the Hebrew Scriptures to look it up, study it, preach it. Here is Moses getting so close to God that he can not only speak to Him as friend to friend, but he can actually touch the face of God and smooth out His angry scowl! Try to imagine it— Moses, stretching out his hands and stroking the face of God till all the wrinkles and frowns are gone!

No, it was not an easy prayer. It was not a matter of withdrawing into a prayer closet for an hour. It was not a day or two of prayer and fasting and then preaching a sermon or writing a book about it. It was forty days—the second forty days in a row. What a wreck Moses' body must have been! But after hearing about the golden calf, he decided the only hope for his nation—the *only* hope—was to persuade God to change His mind.

In Deuteronomy 9:25–27 (NLT) Moses tells the Israelites how he actually did that:

> I fell down and lay before the Lord for forty days and nights when he was ready to destroy you. I prayed to the Lord and said, "O Sovereign Lord, do not destroy your own people. They are your special possession, redeemed from Egypt by your mighty power and glorious strength.

Overlook the stubbornness and sin of these people, but remember instead your servants Abraham, Isaac, and Jacob. . . ."

I realize that after going through the account of Moses' prayers for Israel, no one will expect easily or cheaply to become an intercessor. Imagine Moses, skinny as could be, prostrate on his belly, bare hands and feet resting painfully on the rocks and dust of the Arab ground, hissing snakes slithering around him, scorpions skittering about looking for an opening to assault his exhausted body at the exposed parts—his hands and feet. What a way to pray to God! Forty days. Forty nights.

Oblivious to the world around him, Moses had only one consuming burden: *I've got to get through to God. I've got to take away the anger. I must convince Him to change His mind!*

What sustained him? That same deep desire he expressed to his people when he said, "Maybe I can make atonement for your sin" (Exodus 32:30). Nothing else would do.

Some of you will say to me here, "But what about Calvary?" Calvary had not happened yet, but the principle was the same. Moses, the true intercessor, offered his own life as a sacrifice to make an atonement for his people. He was willing to be punished for their sake. "Please forgive their sin," he begged God, "—and if not, then blot me out of the record you are keeping" (Exodus 32:32, NLT).

Incredible prayer! Do we realize that the two greatest intercessors in the Old and New Testaments, Moses and the apostle Paul, both prayed the same kind of prayer (see

Romans 9:3)? They were willing to give up their own standing before God if only their brothers and sisters could be forgiven. No, they did not say petulantly, "I don't want to go to heaven if You don't save my people." There was no thread of rebellion in their prayers but a deep love and willingness to suffer with Christ on behalf of sinful humans.

That is intercession. And that is what we must do today, more than anything else, if we are to see real change in our world. Yes, the atoning sacrifice of Jesus Christ was complete and sufficient to redeem all mankind, but He calls us to "love each other in the same way that I love you. And here is how to measure it—the greatest love is shown when people lay down their lives for their friends" (John 15:12–13, NLT). Moses did this, and as a result God changed His plans to destroy His people.

The Lord may not change His mind as a human does, but He does change the world—and us—when we pray as Moses did. This is something a superficial Christian can never dream of doing, because he is not willing to pay the price.

The question, then, is, Are we willing? Are we willing to let God be God and to become the men and women He wants us to be? God is looking today for another Moses, another Paul, another man or woman willing to love in the same way they loved, laying down our lives for our friends in prayer.

For the sake of a lost world, to the glory of His name, for the coming of His Kingdom and because you and I are part of the Body of Christ worldwide, let us embrace our role and act on it!

God bless you.

1
We Are Not Helpless!

Some time ago I heard two Christian women discussing the plight of hostages being held by Middle Eastern terrorists.

"I feel sorry for those poor men and their families," one of the women remarked, "but really, this is God's problem, not ours. We have to remember that He has already decided how their stories are going to turn out."

The other woman sighed. "Yes," she said, "but it's frustrating! It seems we're all being held hostage by the evil people in the world—the terrorists and dictators, the drug dealers, the criminals. . . ."

The first woman smiled and patted her friend's arm. "Well, that's how it *looks*," she said comfortingly, "but we know God has His reasons for allowing these things.

Even when we don't understand those reasons, we can be sure that *nothing* happens outside His will."

As I listened, I felt indignation rising within me. I could barely control the urge to turn to them and say, "What's the matter with you? Why are you talking this way? You're not helpless! God has given you the power to change that situation! Why don't you use it? Why don't you pray?"

But sometimes I know when it's pointless to open my mouth, and this was one of those times. Those women wouldn't have understood what I wanted to say. Even so, I couldn't get them out of my mind, and their conversation continued to trouble me because it illustrated perfectly a problem that has caused a tremendous weakening of the Body of Christ in our time.

Those two very devout women were steeped in a false doctrine that has infected the thinking of an alarming number of Christians in our time. I call it—for lack of a better term—*Christian fatalism.* Without realizing it, those women had succumbed to a spiritual error that had all but neutralized their effectiveness as believers. If I had asked them, "My dear ladies, have you considered joining Islam?", no doubt they would have been outraged and offended. But the truth is, their beliefs about "God's will" would have fit very nicely into the Muslim religion, and into a number of other fatalistic religions, too, like Hinduism and Buddhism. There is, however, *no* place for fatalism in Christianity. Quite the opposite!

The Bible is full of powerful illustrations that prove it. In these pages we will highlight a number of them, because I believe that in our determination to submit to the sovereign will of God, too many of us have lost sight of a powerful truth: God never created us to be puppets. He made us in His own image, endowing us with the ability to make independent choices. In doing so, He in a sense restricted His own omnipotence by allowing us to say yes or no to His will.

In other words, God has given us the privilege of choosing how our lives (and our world) will turn out. And those of us who know God are elevated to a stunning position within this framework: We become God's partners and collaborators in writing the story of mankind. Not only that, but we are empowered to challenge the powers of evil that have been at war with God since the beginning of time. We can, through our own faith and our prayers, lift the world off its hinges—if only we *will!*

No, God isn't interested in puppets; He is looking for people who will say yes to His invitation and make a difference in the world. He is looking for people who understand that in making Himself susceptible to our influence, He has given us "the keys of the kingdom" (Matthew 16:19)—the power to change human history for the better.

"Anyone who has faith in me will do what I have been doing," Jesus said. "He will do even greater things than these, because I am going to the Father. And I will do whatever you ask in my name, so that the Son may bring glory to the Father. You may ask me for anything in my name, and I will do it" (John 14:12–14). He couldn't make a more explicit statement, could He? "Take up My cause!" Jesus is saying. "Look at what I have done, and do more! I have given you the power, so go for it!"

But still we hesitate. Still we don't believe it's our place to "tell God what we want Him to do with His world"—which is the way I recently heard a Christian man describe intercessory prayer. But why not? God invites us—even commands us—to do it! Shall we decline His invitation like good Muslims or Buddhists or Hindus, who out of false humility cringe at the thought of a God who is open to influence, whose plans can be changed? I pray that we will not, because God is depending on us—and so is our world. Unless we shake off our fatalistic apathy and use the power God makes available to us through prayer, the blood of many on this planet will be on our hands. We are responsible!

Yes, God wants us to be active, not passive. He wants us to resist—and ultimately defeat—the principalities and powers that have been holding the world hostage since the beginning of recorded history. And He gives us weapons more powerful than theirs to do it. "Whatever you bind on earth will be bound in heaven," Jesus declares, "and whatever you loose on earth will be loosed in heaven" (Matthew 16:19).

Incredible! The fatalist can only shudder at such words! But as Christians we should be electrified by them. They confirm that God has given us access to the unlimited power of Jesus Christ Himself—power far greater than that of any so-called "superpower" on earth. They also tell us that, contrary to what the two women I mentioned earlier believed, God has *not* "already decided how this story will turn out," any more than He has decided whom we will marry or what Gorbachev will be doing five years from today.

Mind you, I'm not saying that God has no plans for us, or that He has taken His hands off the world and is letting us spin out of control into our own self-made oblivion. Nor am I saying that we have ultimate control over God or that He has put us in charge of everything. He is a sovereign God, and we can and should know His will—and we should *do* it. Doing things God's way should always be our objective, and the Scriptures give us all the guidelines necessary for that task. But we must also remember that God's plans for us are not chiseled in concrete. Only His character and nature are unchanging; His decisions are not!

Yes, when we see things happening in the world that appear to be "acts of God," and we disagree with what God seems to be doing (or allowing), *we can ask Him to change His mind.* God is always ready to listen to our side of the story, and even if He has made plans to do something, He is open to changing those plans under the right conditions.

Moses understood this facet of God's character as few men ever have, and the Bible gives us plenty of examples to help us understand how we can relate to God the way he did. In Exodus we read that the Lord said to Moses, "I have seen what a stubborn, rebellious lot these people are. . . . My anger shall blaze out against them and destroy them all." Sounds pretty final, doesn't it? A fatalist might have responded, "Oh, boy, we're in for it now! It's all over!" But Moses didn't accept that. He "begged God not to do it. . . . So the Lord changed his mind and spared them" (Exodus 32:9, 11,14, LB).

Moses knew it was possible to change God's mind, just as most of the other heroes of the Bible did. Moses *knew God*, and as God's friend he understood that God's plans could be changed. In later chapters we will talk more about Moses and the others who changed God's mind, but for now it's enough to know that these were human beings just like you and me, and if they could change God's mind, so can we! It happens all the time.

One example that particularly thrills me involves the recent developments in the Soviet Union. Back in 1983 our organization, Open Doors, called for seven years of prayer for the Soviet Union. We were convinced that the evil conspiracy that had brought untold misery and torment to the Body of Christ worldwide was headquartered in one place: Moscow. Millions had died as a result of genocide in Communist nations, and hundreds of thousands were in prison for their faith. We decided to take the offensive against Satan by attacking his strongholds. Many Christians around the world joined us. We prayed particularly that the barriers that have kept God's Word out of Eastern Europe and Russia would be removed and that Christian prisoners would be set free.

Within a year we began to see results. We heard for

the first time about an obscure man named Gorbachev. We began to hear the words *glasnost* and *perestroika* instead of the usual Communist rhetoric. The winds of change we prayed for began to blow, and there was no holding them back. Finally, just under six years from the time we first began praying, the walls between East and West began to crumble. The Berlin Wall—a worldwide symbol of Communist oppression—came tumbling down. Prison doors began to open. Eastern Europe rose up against the powers that had held them in bondage.

In 1989, after more than thirty years of smuggling Bibles behind the Iron Curtain, I challenged the Russians openly to allow our organization to distribute a million Russian-language Bibles to Soviet churches. Incredibly, they said yes. And at this moment, still less than seven years after we began praying, we are able to report to our prayer partners the glorious news that *not a single Christian leader remains in a prison or concentration camp in the Soviet Union for his faith!* That, my friend, is what happens when we pray.

Yes, we do have something to say about the things that happen around us. We don't have to take life as it comes; we can have an earth-shaking impact on our world because God's mind and heart are open to us and His power is available to us. It's no wonder God gets exasperated when He sees how reluctant we are to use the power of prayer. "This is a people plundered and despoiled," He says in Isaiah. "All of them are trapped in caves, or are hidden away in prisons; they have become a prey with none to deliver them, and a spoil, with none to say, 'Give them back!' Who among you will give ear to this?" (Isaiah 42:22–23, NASB). Who, indeed? Who will stand up to Satan in our time and demand, as Moses did before Pharaoh, "Let My people go" (Exodus 7:16, NASB)? Who will be on the Lord's side?

Certainly it will not be the fatalists—Christian or otherwise. They will never challenge the powers that be. It should worry us that Islam is the fastest-growing religion on earth. The majority of the people on this planet today, in fact, belong to the fatalistic non-Christian religions, and their numbers are increasing at an alarming rate. And now the Christian Church is being infected as well with the paralyzing virus of fatalistic apathy. How can this be?

It isn't so hard to understand. There is no denying the appeal of fatalism to people who are "spiritually inclined"—people who long to be religious. The fatalist's attitude seems to reflect tremendous faith: "I refuse to question the will of God," he will say with pious humility. But does he actually mean that whatever happens in the world is all right with him—including war, famine, oppression, the breakdown of the family and society, the exploitation of the innocent and weak, the degradation of all that is holy and pure? "If God allows it, there must be a reason," he will say, "and I can't hope to understand God's reasons with my small mind, so I accept what He does by faith and 'praise the Lord anyway.' " And ignorant listeners to this kind of talk will respond admiringly, "What faith!"

This kind of "faith" has no power, however, because it is based on a false premise. Call it what you like—*karma*, destiny, fate, *kismet*—it amounts to the same thing regardless of the costume it wears. It says that we cannot change the script God has written and our duty is merely to "go with the flow" of God's program. It makes life so simple, doesn't it? Yes, and that's a good part of its appeal. Fatalists can relax because they are no longer responsible for anything. They don't have to obey God or actively resist evil; they can simply "let it be" (as the Beatles recommended in their hit song of the '60s).

Fatalism has other appeals as well. If a Christian can incorporate fatalism into his theology, his life becomes immeasurably easier and more comfortable. He will gain hundreds of extra hours each year for television viewing and napping when he no longer has to waste time on such fruitless activities as studying the Scriptures, getting to know God through prayer, interceding for his family and for the world, combating the forces of evil or reaching out to others for the sake of Christ. He won't have to lift a finger again. He can sit in his recliner and vegetate for the rest of his life, feeling perfectly secure in his "faith." He is ready to meet every calamity of life, from divorce to death, with an attitude of stoic acceptance.

There is nothing new about this, of course. Even some of the greatest heroes in the Bible succumbed occasionally to fatalism. Remember what Job said upon learning that his whole family had been wiped out and everything he owned was lost? "The Lord gave and the Lord has taken away. Blessed be the name of the Lord" (Job 1:21, NASB). Astonishing! What a statement! Indeed, it is these words that are often quoted at funerals today as an affirmation of faith in the face of devastating loss.

But is this attitude Christian? No! It is "scriptural" only in the sense that the words are found in the Bible. What we must recognize is that these words were uttered in absolute ignorance by a man who had no idea that God and Satan were using his body as a battleground. Job couldn't see that Satan was counting on fatalism as his most potent weapon.

But we can't be too hard on Job; he didn't have the Bible to help him understand God's character or the nature of the spiritual warfare that was taking place in his life. He had no way of knowing that it was Satan, not God, who had "taken away" everything he held dear. The miracle of Job's story is not that he accepted his suffering without question; it is that in spite of his mistaken ideas about who was causing it, he still refused to curse God or charge Him with wrongdoing. So we can admire Job for remaining faithful in spite of his misconceptions about the situation. But we have no business transforming his misconceptions into Christian theology!

Our response to Satan's devious tactics should reflect a far deeper knowledge of God than Job's, because we have not only the Scriptures to draw upon, but two thousand years of Christian experience as well. We also have the Holy Spirit to enlighten us. But too many Christians today are in the same boat with those two women I heard talking about the hostages. They are drifting along, contentedly going with the flow as though the revelation of God ceased during Job's era, the Holy Spirit never came and prayer was never given to us as a way of gaining access to the heart and mind of God. Sadly, they don't realize until it is too late that the current that seems to be offering a comfortable, secure ride is actually pulling them faster and faster toward a deadly whirlpool—and oblivion.

This has been one of Satan's fundamental strategies throughout history. He continues to employ it because it has worked so well for so long. But we cannot permit his strategy to succeed! We have the power to resist and overcome him, and God has placed the weapon in our hands that can do so. That weapon is prayer.

Nothing makes Satan quite so fearful as a Christian who understands the power of prayer, because he knows that God holds nothing back from His friends. As we know God and begin to understand all that He is and all that is His, we are no longer helpless victims who can be tossed about by the storms and waves Satan stirs up. We are, in fact, capable of doing what the devil and his demons cannot. Jesus tells us,

> "If you have faith and do not doubt . . . you can say to this mountain, 'Go, throw yourself into the sea,' and it will be done. If you believe, you will receive whatever you ask for in prayer." Matthew 21:21–22

21

No wonder Satan is desperate to keep Christians from serious prayer! He has no power compared to that. Through prayer, not only can we move mountains, we can defeat every one of Satan's evil plans. It is a life-and-death matter, you see—for Satan as well as for us. It should not surprise us, then, that he works overtime dreaming up schemes to neutralize our prayers. If he can do that, he has nothing to fear from us. He can pursue his unholy agenda unhindered.

This is why I am concerned about Christian fatalism. It is not merely an innocuous doctrinal interpretation that we can coexist with as we do in the case of minor variations in Christian theology. Fatalism is a paralyzing disease that has invaded the Body of Christ with disastrous consequences. It infects its victims with complacency and apathy that immobilize their will to resist evil while eroding their determination to accomplish the great work of Christ.

Unless this creeping paralytic disease is halted, the world is going to be in even more desperate trouble than it already is. The ultimate cost in terms of human suffering will be horrifying beyond our comprehension. The atrocities and oppression we saw in Hitler's Europe, Mao's China and Stalin's Russia will pale by comparison. Millions will continue to languish in isolation and despair all around the globe at a time when they ought to be able to count on us to come to their rescue. And if we believe for a moment that God will keep the evil that is engulfing the rest of humanity away from our doorsteps, we are tragically mistaken. He will do no such thing. If we hide from the truth by taking refuge in false doctrines, we deserve to experience the consequences. Believe me, God will not protect us from them. We are not exempt from suffering.

Make no mistake: Satan is not getting nicer or more genteel as time goes on. (We will look at his strategies and how to counter them in chapters 6 and 7.) He is becoming stronger and more monstrous every day. We have only to look at current headlines to know that. A friend of mine put it this way: "When I was young, a bad boy was someone who swiped an apple from the grocer. Now a bad boy is someone who murders his whole family so he can collect insurance money to buy drugs."

We all know this is no exaggeration. The boundaries of evil are expanding every day, and fatalistic apathy is enabling those boundaries to grow because it offers no resistance. But Christians *must* oppose evil; we were born for battle! Every Christian is a soldier, a "member of the resistance" in God's army, taking part in spiritual warfare. The moment we lose sight of this, we become aimless in our actions and fuzzy in our focus. We forget why we were born, forget what we have been trained and equipped to do on the battlefield, and we die without ever knowing why we lived. Most importantly, we never complete the mission we were sent to accomplish. Score one more for the devil.

You see, once we begin to understand the consequences of Christian fatalism, we can no longer tolerate it. We must fight it for all we are worth, because it is the most powerful weapon the enemy is using at this moment in history to defeat the purposes of God.

So where does this leave us? Is the situation hopeless? Or is it possible to reverse the paralysis that threatens the Body of Christ, regain the ground we have lost by default and turn back the enemy? It will not be easy, but I am convinced it can be done. This book will outline the steps we must take if we are going to do it. It will give you the knowledge you need to take the offensive against the powers of darkness—and win.

But I should warn you: Knowledge can be a dangerous thing. By the time you have finished this book, you will know things that will require something of you. You will be compelled to take action. You will pray and mountains will move. You will use the keys to the Kingdom to open prison doors and set men free; you will strike back at the enemy who has held the world hostage too long. This will place you in the thick of the spiritual battle for planet earth in ways you may not have experienced before. You may become a target for the devil's attacks in ways you cannot imagine at this moment. Your life will never be the same again, that I can promise you.

So if you are looking for a peaceful, predictable life, it might be better if you closed this book right now and gave it away to someone who is after a little excitement. Remember what Jesus said: "I did not come to bring peace, but a sword" (Matthew 10:34). Be prepared! If you finish this book and apply the knowledge it imparts, if you learn how to discern when God's mind is open to change, and if you believe He is waiting for our prayers in order to defeat the enemy, then all prospects for a conventional life will be gone forever. You will take up the sword of the Spirit and perform great exploits for God, fulfilling His eternal purpose in ways nobody else can. In the next chapter we will look at exactly how you can prepare to do this.

I ask you, my friend: How will you be remembered in history? Will your name be spoken in the same reverent tones as those of Abraham, Moses, David, Joshua, Elijah or Paul? Will you "subdue kingdoms" through your prayers? Or will you fade into obscurity without ever living up to your high calling in God?

The choice is yours.

2
Who Can Change God's Mind?

Have you ever wondered why most Christians today are not doing the "greater things" that Jesus said we would do? For that matter, why we are not even doing the *same* things Jesus did? We call ourselves Christians—meaning "little Christs"—but do we love as Jesus loved, live as He lived and, above all, pray as He prayed, and with the same earth-shaking results? I'm not talking about miracles now—it's obvious that most of us don't routinely raise the dead, restore sight to the blind or satisfy several thousand hungry people with five loaves of bread and a couple of fish. I'm only asking whether or not we are making the kind of difference in the world that Jesus said we should make, the kind of difference the apostles and early Christians made.

There are exceptions, of course, but I think we can agree that most Christians today are not. The reason is simple: We don't understand that we can have the kind of relationship with God that will produce such results. We don't believe God will do what we ask because we don't really understand who He is or the principles that guide our relationship with Him.

Strong words? Perhaps. But if we understood God as the prophets and apostles and early believers did, if we really knew how to pray, wouldn't we be doing the greater things that Jesus predicted? If we knew God as He wants us to know Him, we would automatically have all the faith required to pray with the unlimited power and authority of Jesus Christ. Nothing would be impossible to us.

But year after year, decade after decade, people who do things "the Jesus way" seem fewer and farther between. The prayer link between the Body of Christ and the Godhead has grown weaker instead of stronger. Our prayers, too, have often degenerated into tedious recitations of "wish lists" instead of exciting, two-way dialogues and strategic planning sessions with the Creator of the universe. We are not convinced that anything will happen when we pray, so it doesn't. No wonder we look for excuses to avoid it! Would any of us willingly spend even a few minutes a day with a friend who never responded to anything we said, and never lifted a finger to help us when we needed it?

Our God *does* respond, however, when we understand how to talk with Him. He will move heaven and earth for every one of us, just as He did for Moses and Elijah, if we grasp the scriptural principles that make it possible. Even today we can look around us and observe some Christians whose lives reflect the intimacy of their relationship with God. They pray and things happen! They're not surprised. They know what God can do, and they have enough confidence in Him to ask for big things and expect an answer. But such individuals are rare these days, aren't they? We have reached the point at which people living as Jesus told us to live are nothing less than spectacles to the rest of us. We would probably call them fanatics, meaning that they love Jesus more than we do.

We are stunned by the dramatic answers to prayer described in the Bible stories of the prophets and apostles, and we are inspired by modern examples like those experienced by my old friend Corrie ten Boom, who amidst the horrors of a Nazi concentration camp became one of our generation's most effective and irresistible prayer warriors. (I can remember praying with Corrie and thinking, *This is a woman God could never refuse!*)

The problem is that we see such people as *different* from ourselves. We imagine that they have a special gift that sets them apart from ordinary Christians like us. We place them on pedestals and call them "spiritual giants" and "heroes of faith," and, indeed, they are in one sense. But we miss the point: They are not different from us at all. They simply understand one idea crucial to intercession: The people who change God's mind are the people who know two things about Him—His character and His will.

God's Character

One episode from Moses' dealings with the children of Israel helps us understand how knowing God's character can affect our prayers.

As Exodus 32–34 opens, we find Moses and the people of Israel in an unbelievable situation. While Moses is up on Mount Sinai receiving God's handwritten instructions, the Israelites waiting for him in the valley below decide they have been waiting long enough. They demand that Aaron make them other gods to worship, so he melts down earrings collected from the people to create a golden calf.

Meanwhile, as God concludes His instructions to Moses, He reveals that the Israelites, "a stiff-necked people," have been "quick to turn away" from His commandments and are worshiping a golden calf. Compounding their sin, they are even crediting the idol with leading them out of bondage in Egypt!

Understandably, God's patience has finally run out. He declares that He has made up His mind to destroy Israel. "Now leave me alone," God tells Moses, "so that my anger may burn against them and that I may destroy them" (Exodus 32:10). But notice that God finishes this statement with the words, "Then I will make you into a great nation."

This declaration presents Moses with a difficult personal choice. God is offering him the opportunity to really become *somebody!* Instead of being stuck with this bunch of ingrates and infidels who turn their backs on

God at every opportunity, Moses can start fresh and become the patriarch of a great nation. How many of us would say no to such an offer from God? *After all,* we might tell ourselves, *if God wants to wipe out these rebellious wretches and use me to build a nation that will glorify Him, who am I to argue?*

But Moses, the true intercessor, doesn't accept *a* word from the Lord as *the* word from the Lord. He understands God's character; he knows God to be reasonable, merciful and true to His word. So he says to the Lord, in effect, "God, You can't do this! What will the Egyptians say if they hear You've destroyed the very people You called Your own and led out of captivity? And besides, don't You remember Your servants Abraham, Isaac and Israel? What about the things You promised them? You can't go back on Your word!"

Now there is a man who knows how to pray with insight and authority! As a result, God mercifully "change[s] His mind and spare[s] them" (Exodus 32:14, LB).

But the story doesn't end here. After convincing God to give the Israelites one more chance, Moses comes down from the mountain—with God's handwritten Law under his arm—to find his people dancing naked before the golden calf. In a fit of outrage or perhaps in a futile attempt to destroy the accusation against them (of which he holds the only copy in his hands), he shatters the tablets of the Law and demands that Aaron explain how he could possibly lead the people into such terrible sin. Aaron's reply will surely go down in history as one of the most astonishing examples of quick thinking ever recorded.

"You know how prone these people are to evil," he tells Moses. "They said to me, 'Make us gods who will go before us.'. . . So I told them, 'Whoever has any gold jewelry, take it off.' Then they gave me the gold, and I threw it into the fire, and out came this calf!" (Exodus 32:22–24).

Now you have to give Aaron credit. On a moment's notice he is able to turn idolatry and debauchery into a miracle of God!

Amazingly, it is after this stunning confrontation that Moses goes back to God and prays the boldest prayer ever recorded (equaled only by the apostle Paul's prayer for Israel in Romans 9:3) in an attempt to make atonement for his people.

"Oh, what a great sin these people have committed!" he tells the Lord. "But now, please forgive their sin— but if not, then blot me out of the book you have written" (Exodus 32:31–32). Incredible! This time Moses takes a gigantic leap of faith. In essence he says, "God, I understand Your righteousness and I know something about atonement. I'm going to offer the only atonement for my people that might be acceptable to You. Here am I; blot me out of Your book instead of them."

Moses is not defying God. He isn't saying, as some have contended, "Lord, if You don't want Israel, You can't have me either." No, Moses presents himself as an atoning sacrifice for the sins of his people. He offers to do what Jesus will do. He acts and speaks by revelation, and with such perfect insight into God's character and purposes that hundreds of years later, God chooses Moses to go with Elijah to the Mount of Transfiguration and speak with Jesus about what His atoning death in Jerusalem will accomplish (Luke 9:30–31). So you see, in interceding for his nation instead of accepting God's plans as final, Moses changes history in more ways than one!

God's response to Moses' offer of atonement is this: "Who ever has sinned against me I will blot out of my book" (Exodus 32:33). The Israelites will have to pay the penalty their sin requires. Still, for Moses' sake, God does not utterly destroy them.

In the period that follows, Moses and God grow closer and closer. "The Lord would speak to Moses face to face, as a man speaks with his friend" (Exodus 33:11). What an astounding statement! Moses and God are talking things over just as you and I might at my front door!

In one of these conversations, Moses approaches God with a remarkable request: "If I have found favor in your eyes, teach me your ways so I may know you. . . . Remember that this nation is your people" (Exodus 33:13). Moses knows, of course, that he has found grace in God's sight. God would hardly be talking with him every day if he had not! So Moses appeals to God as his friend. He can ask God for *anything*, and predictably he asks for the one thing that matters most to him as Israel's faithful intercessor: "Help me to know You better," he asks, "so I can continue to be Your friend and ensure that this nation is truly Your people."

God responds to Moses' plea with a verbal embrace: "I will do the very thing you have asked, because I am pleased with you and I know you by name" (Exodus 33:17). This beautiful affirmation prompts Moses to ask one more big thing. It is something no one has ever asked of God before: "Now show me your glory" (Exodus 33:18). Or, as one scholar translates it: "Show me *Thine own self!*" (Helen Spurrell). Can you imagine how it must have touched God's heart that Moses would make such a remarkable request? God responds without hesitation: "I will cause all my goodness to pass in front of you, and I will proclaim my name, the Lord, in your presence" (Exodus 33:19).

Yes, God gives Moses what He has never given any man: There on Mount Sinai the Lord Jehovah passes "all His goodness" before Moses, hiding nothing but His face, for Moses' own protection—"for no one may see me and live" (Exodus 33:20). As this spectacle progresses God announces who He is, giving us another stunning view of His character: "The Lord, the Lord, the compassionate and gracious God, slow to anger, abounding in love and faithfulness, maintaining love to thousands, and forgiving wickedness, rebellion and sin" (Exodus 34:6–7).

Again God reveals His character by telling Moses the meaning of His name, which is God's way of saying, "Moses, you asked to know Me; this is what I am like:

—Tenderly compassionate, kind, understanding
—Patient, reasonable, slow to anger

—Faithful and true

—Righteous and just."

But God further expands Moses' understanding by announcing Himself with a doubly emphatic name, "The Lord, The Lord" (which can also be translated "The eternal God, Ruler of all things"). This reminds Moses of God's sovereign power and authority.

How does Moses respond to this stunning revelation of God? Predictably, the great intercessor loses no time in putting his new knowledge to work for his people. "God," he says, in essence, "when You call Yourself by these names and I see who You are, it gives me hope that You might forgive even the unforgivable sins of my people! So I ask You—in spite of everything—to restore us and make us Your own!" This is surely one of the most brilliant strategic prayers of all time.

It is also one of the most effective: "I am making a covenant with you," God replies to Moses. "Before all your people I will do wonders never before done in any nation in all the world. The people you live among will see how awesome is the work that I, the Lord, will do for you" (Exodus 34:10).

Do you understand what is happening here? Moses appeals to God out of a profound understanding of His revealed character, and God responds instantly by giving Moses everything he asks, and much more. He also gives the Israelites what they do not deserve—another chance.

Let's look at the things we know about God from this one small portion of Scripture. We know that God is not only the holy, sovereign, eternal King, but He is also our loving Father—fair, just, compassionate, forgiving and true to His Word. We see, too, that God does not want to hurt or destroy His people; He goes to incredible lengths to avoid it, forgiving not just once or twice, but "seventy times seven" before His righteousness finally demands payment of the penalty for sin. Nobody has ever been able to say to God, "You didn't give me a chance!" God always gives us more chances than we deserve to turn from sin and become His friends.

We see also that before anything else, an understanding of God's character and purposes is essential to everything we do in the spiritual realm. The answer to the question "Who is God?" is the basis of all prayer, because we cannot relate to God in anything but a superficial way until we know who He is.

When you begin any acquaintance, the first thing you do is observe and ask questions about the other person's personality and character. What is he like? Is he relaxed and patient or a finger-drummer and a toe-tapper? Is he rigid or open to new ideas? Does he listen with interest and respect or would he prefer to perform monologues? Does he meet you halfway or does he want a give-and-take relationship in which you do a hundred percent of the giving while he does a hundred percent of the taking? Does he make fair and reasonable judgments about people or does he condemn others regardless of circumstances? Is he kind or harsh? Can you believe what he says or does he exaggerate and mislead you, making promises he has no intention of keeping?

By asking questions like these, we decide how much potential there is for friendship. We build a foundation of assumptions upon which the relationship can continue. We can't be friends with someone who is totally unpredictable and unreliable. We have certain needs and expectations, and when those aren't met, it isn't possible to build a healthy or satisfying relationship. We must question and probe to find out the reasons this person behaves as he does, because those reasons will explain what we can expect in the future. When we don't understand something we ask, "Why did you do that? What were you thinking?" We stretch to comprehend guiding principles so we can anticipate how our friend is going to react to us and to the world. This is, of course, the same process we should follow to build our friendship with God.

What do we know about God? How does He act? What has He done before? How does He describe Himself? What is our experience with Him? These are essential questions that must be addressed before we can hope to influence Him through prayer.

Ask a Muslim, "Who is God?" and he'll answer by reciting a list of 99 attributes of God—not one of which is *Father*. That is another fundamental difference between our God and the gods worshiped by every religion on earth. The Christian can call God "Father," because Jesus told us that's who He is: our Father. He is even more than Father, however; He is *Abba*—the Hebrew language version of "Daddy" or "Papa." Our God is the Daddy into whose lap we can climb, like little children, knowing He loves us unreservedly.

So that's one answer to the question "Who is God?" God is not only *a* Father, He is *our Daddy*. But what else do we know about Him? The many-faceted revelation of God's character in the Scriptures emphasizes several other qualities that make Him different from the gods and "prophets" of any religion. One of the most important, of course, is that He is loving. We are creatures who cannot live without loving and being loved because we were made in the image of God. Our minds, spirits and emotions yearn for the love of God. We can never fully satisfy that yearning outside of God, because "God is love. . . . We love because he first loved us" (1 John 4:16, 19).

God defines Himself as the great Lover of mankind who longs to be loved in return. Dozens of Scriptures reveal the depth and tenderness of God's love for us, including the entire Song of Solomon—the most beautiful love song ever written. God expressed His love through Jeremiah by saying, "I have loved you with an everlasting love; I have drawn you with loving-kindness" (Jeremiah 31:3). He says elsewhere in Jeremiah, "I am the Lord, I show unfailing love, I do justice and right upon the earth; for on these I have set my heart" (Jeremiah 9:24, NEB).

But it isn't just God's words that are loving. His deeds are loving, too. There is no god in the history of mankind other than ours who not only claims to love us, but proved it by laying down His life for us. We can have no doubts about the quality or the limitless quantity of that love. As the saying goes, "I asked Jesus, 'How much do you love me?' and Jesus said, 'This much,' and He stretched out His arms and died."

Many people have taken issue with the idea that a loving God could have created a world in which there is so much pain and misery. That argument has raged for centuries, but Jesus settled it completely when He took our place on the cross. That was God's answer to pain and misery. As Christians we know as well that the pain and misery in this world are not God's doing or His choice. He suffers with us, and ultimately suffered for us, but He never wants to make us suffer. Out of love, He gave us the freedom to say yes or no to His just and righteous will, and to the extent that we've said no, we have permitted the forces of evil to wreak havoc upon our world. The suffering we experience is the natural consequence of ungodly behavior —either our own or that of others. As humans, we are the authors of our own misery. God alone is the author of love.

There are thousands of pieces of evidence in the Scriptures that exemplify God's loving, just, righteous and fatherly character. We can't go into all—or even a fraction—of them here, obviously. But we have seen a number of characteristics that will enable you to relate to God on a more intimate level. Beyond that, you have eternity to explore the unlimited riches of God's personality and Spirit!

There is one more characteristic I want to mention, however, and that is the subtle but extremely important quality of consistency. God proves by His actions that

He *is* all the things He calls Himself. You may find a certain irony in this: On the one hand God is consistent, and on the other—as the Scriptures clearly prove—He can and does change His mind! How can we have it both ways?

There is a profound truth in this apparent irony. God will always act in ways consistent with His revealed character and purposes. These do not change. He is who He is and there is no shadow of turning in Him. But He is at heart a compassionate, loving God open to the needs and desires of those who know Him. In other words, *God's character, nature and purposes are changeless, but His plans are flexible.*

That flexibility gives us the opportunity to alter the course of our world through prayer when we know how to meet God's conditions for change and it leads us now to the subject of His will. When we begin to know Him better, we begin to understand His plans for the world. Then when we follow scriptural guidelines and learn to pray in ways that are consistent with His loving, holy purposes and will, we become involved in carrying out—and sometimes changing—God's plans. This is, in fact, the way we glorify Him and become true participants in His creative work. A look at the prophet Elijah helps us understand how.

God's Will

Perhaps after reading the earlier story of Moses and the children of Israel you still tend to think that he was larger than life, that we could never be like him. Is that so? Then look at how the Scriptures describe this other great Bible hero:

> Elijah was a man just like us. He prayed earnestly that it would not rain, and it did not rain on the land for three and a half years. Again he prayed, and the heavens gave rain, and the earth produced its crops.
>
> James 5:17–18

Read that first sentence once more: He "was a man *just like us*"—subject to all the same types of fears, distractions, problems and doubts. Elijah even had handicaps that we don't: Jesus had not yet appeared on the scene, nor had the Holy Spirit come to empower believers. Yet he prayed and it did not rain for three years. When he prayed again, the rains fell. Why? Because Elijah knew God and understood His will. Thus, when he prayed God changed His mind.

This story, told in 1 Kings 17–18, helps us see the connection between knowing God's will and changing His mind. Let's look at it briefly and see what we learn from the way that unusual drought ended.

First, notice the harmony here between Elijah and God, as if two friends are working to accomplish a divine plan. Elijah had said the rain would come only "at my word" (17:1) and God let him know in the third year that it would soon be time for that word (18:1).

Then we read in 1 Kings 18:41–46 that Elijah was aware of the sound of heavy rain long before a cloud appeared in the sky. His response? Prayer. He "bent down to the

41

ground," began to intercede, and sent his servant seven times to observe the sky in the direction of the sea. Finally a small cloud appeared and a drenching downpour followed.

This suggests to us that because Elijah knew God, he also knew two things: God wanted him to pray for rain and God would not have changed His mind about the drought—that is, ended it—had Elijah not prayed.

Although Elijah knew God's will and the word had already been spoken, it still needed intensive intercession for God to implement His plan. (Did you ever pray with your head between your knees on a rocky floor? Try it!) Failing to see this has brought too much suffering to the world. Where are the Elijahs today who will change God's mind?

Elijah was not "special." His friendship with God was the only thing that made him exceptional. Because of that closeness he knew how to intercede in a way that got results.

Who can change God's mind? Those close to Him, those who know Him well enough to understand His character and His will, those eager to believe that God not only welcomes our prayers to change His mind, but *wants* them. This gives you and me a great opportunity because God is looking today for another Moses or Elijah—men and women who will make friendship with Him the top priority of their lives. We have the same heroic potential—not to do the same work, but to have the same kind of impact on the world that they had because of their prayers.

You see, prayer is not only the great "elevator" that can carry every believer into the presence of the King; it's also the great "equalizer" that gives us equal access to God. Whatever our experiences, intelligence, bank balances, education, social status or family circumstances, you and I have the same access to Him that every "spiritual giant" in history has had. With Moses, Elijah, Abraham, Paul and many others we can share "the treasures of darkness, riches stored in secret places" (Isaiah 45:3) promised by God to His friends. When we are that kind of friend to God, there is no limit to what our prayers can do.

The question is, what are the prerequisites to building this dynamic sort of relationship? There's no mystery about it. As always, God has made the way plain, because He longs to be close to us. If we follow scriptural guidelines for praying according to God's will, we can have a spontaneous, honest, vital communion with Him that knows no boundaries. (We will discuss these guidelines in the next chapter.) Within that framework, we *will* do the greater things that Jesus talked about, through our actions as well as our prayers. We will go to God with tremendous assurance and enthusiasm because we'll know who He is. We will automatically pray "according to His will" because we'll know what His purposes are and discern His will in every situation— and our prayers will reflect it. That's how our relationship with God *should* work!

The apostles and prophets understood this. Every "hero of faith" has been a hero only to the extent that

He has developed true friendship with God. As the apostle Paul wrote to believers in Philippi:

> I consider everything a loss compared to the surpassing greatness of knowing Christ Jesus my Lord, for whose sake I have lost all things. I consider them rubbish. . . . I want to know Christ and the power of his resurrection and the fellowship of sharing in his sufferings, becoming like him in his death.
>
> Philippians 3:8, 10

What a statement! Paul was willing to give everything he had, including his life, so that he might *know Jesus*. That was his number one priority. It was also God's. The result? Today you and I are different people, living in a different world, than would have been the case if Paul had not known the Lord as he did. You see, the prayers of God's friends not only change the individuals who pray; they also have a ripple effect that carries on throughout subsequent history. And, yes, sometimes they change God's mind as well!

I can't stress enough that God doesn't reserve this kind of communication for the "super-spiritual" or those with a special gift. He wants to get through to us in a way we can understand. He has done everything imaginable—and infinitely more—to make that possible. Did you know that every religion in the world has gods that must be sought out by man, while our God is the only one who has come searching for *us*?

Beginning with Adam and Eve in the Garden, God

has always been looking for us instead of waiting for us to find Him. In the greatness of His love, He has always made the first move. He has called out to us through the prophets, made Himself accessible through Jesus Christ and, finally, sent the Holy Spirit to help us achieve perfect harmony and fellowship with Him. Our God relentlessly seeks closer union with us. We have only to respond to His offer of intimacy.

"Let not the wise man boast of his wisdom," the Lord says, "or the strong man boast of his strength or the rich man boast of his riches, but let him who boasts boast about this: that he understands and knows me" (Jeremiah 9:23–24).

Let me tell you a story, and I pray that this illustration is the right one. Not that the alternative is wrong—no, but it is painful. I can only get hurt to the extent that I let you into my heart. And isn't that also where we can hurt God?

Years ago, before anyone had joined me on my long journeys in Communist countries, I began to ask God for a wife and family. I felt then that a family would be an antidote to the loneliness that followed every long and hazardous trip.

God's answer, several times, was clear and unmistakable: "More are the children of the desolate than the children of the married" (see Isaiah 54:1).

I wasn't content with that answer, so I continued to pray, asking God to give me a wife and children. And God answered, bringing me a wife and five great kids who love the Lord and are serving Him. I received what

I asked, despite God's initial "no" answer (if I may call it that).

It's only now, in retrospect, that I can look back over these years and understand why God at first refused me. Only He knew the almost unbearable pain and suffering a family could bring me in the years ahead. Only He could see that they could become, in a very real sense, *burdens* that I had to carry on my dangerous and extended trips. My concern for "the folks at home" would create untold misery. Homesickness—which I had never experienced before—would plague me wherever I went.

Added to that would be the misery and anxiety my family experienced during my prolonged absences. Much of the time while my children were growing up I was far away, out of touch, unavailable even by telephone or postal service. When family crises arose, my wife had to handle them without my support or involvement. And because of the nature of my work, I have had to do the same.

Even now, as I write this, I am in the Shouf Mountains in Lebanon, surrounded by hundreds of gun-toting Druzes. I have just finished lunch with Walid Jumblatt, the undisputed leader of all the Druzes, in his palace. Nobody knows I am here, and I can share it with no one.

And I realize more than ever that intimacy with the Lord Jesus is the one thing that will make our lives count as they should count.

3
Asking According to God's Will

Now that we know the importance of intimacy in praying to change God's mind, we can begin to learn more and more about His will. The important thing is to grow in confidence that we know His will—and can even know when to ask Him to change His mind.

I have found, oddly, that the ones who question knowing God's will the most are the ones who are least likely to move forward in this area—particularly about issues on which God's will is stated clearly in the Bible. They ask two questions, and these questions seem to come up almost everywhere I speak on the subject of prayer: "How can I know God's will?" and "How can I be sure I am praying according to His will?" When I hear them I always suppress a little sigh, because I know that most of the time what people are really saying is, "I'm waiting for God to telegraph instructions from heaven before I do something in the spiritual realm."

It's all too easy to use our ignorance of God's will as an excuse for doing nothing. "I would go on the mission field," many Christians have told me, "if only I could be sure it's God's will." When somebody says this to me, I reply, "All right, then, I'll *tell* you what God's will is: 'Go ye.' Now—will you go?"

Sadly, they won't! When I say that, the response is usually a flustered, "Oh, I know Jesus said that, but how can I be sure this is God's will for me personally? After all, there are a lot of factors involved in this decision. I'd have to give up my job, and my children would be uprooted. And where would we go, exactly? It's dangerous in a lot of countries now, and I couldn't expose my family to that. No, before I could do something that drastic I'd need to have a word from the Lord saying it was His will for *me*."

The people who respond this way aren't really much interested in God's will, I suspect, because if they were, they would be out doing it instead of holding out for a more comfortable alternate. They've simply found a way to get around God's will while still sounding spiritual. After all, what could sound more spiritual than "I'm not going to make a move until God shows me it's His perfect will"? We could use that as an excuse to avoid doing almost anything.

"I would pay my taxes," a man might say, "but first I have to be sure it's God's will. Perhaps God would prefer that I give the money to the church, or use it for my family." If he did that, of course, the government would soon make all his decisions for him! But we who know God would never say such a thing in the first place, because we know what Jesus taught: "Give to Caesar what is Caesar's" (Mark 12:17). We know His will without having to ask Him to reveal it again every year. There may be rare exceptions to the rule, but normally we can act upon God's expressed will without waiting for new or revised instructions from heaven. God has spoken, and His character and principles are eternally the same. We can stake our lives on them.

Many Christians these days still don't understand this. They're always "waiting on the Lord" for a revelation of His will when—especially in the larger issues like evangelism or intercession—His will is already perfectly clear. And they will probably wait forever, because the dramatic revelation they are seeking isn't going to come. This will, of course, give them the excuse they need to avoid doing what they really don't want to do to begin with.

Harsh words? No, I think they are accurate. We need to recognize apathy and laziness if we're going to remove them from our lives and do what God has commanded us to do. God never intended that we should live in a state of suspended animation, forever waiting for a word from Him about what to do next. His purposes and will are not mysteries. In most cases, we can—and should—know them, as we know Him. He and His will are inseparable.

Think of it this way: We instinctively know what will please our human parents, don't we? We know the principles that guide them, know what they approve and disapprove of. We understand the rules, like: "You will never hit your sister" or "You will always speak respectfully to your parents." Beyond these specific rules, we also know the general principles we have learned from daily experience in our family. As children in school, for example, we didn't have to stop every five minutes and run to our parents to ask, "Now, is it your will for me to study today's arithmetic lesson? Should I finish the problems our teacher assigned?"

We didn't have to worry about things like that. We knew the principles our parents taught us, and we could assume from what we already knew that we were supposed to study hard and finish today's arithmetic lesson. Because we knew our parents, we knew what to do from hour to hour without asking constantly, "Is this really what you want?" Certain principles prevail, so we could act using those principles as guideposts. And we could feel sure that our parents would be pleased when we acted accordingly.

This gives children tremendous security. Without this basic knowledge, we would grow up at loose ends, too afraid of making the wrong decisions to make any decisions at all. We would be totally neutralized and incapable of making our way through life because we could never be sure if our actions would meet with our parents' approval or bring a reprimand. We would spend most of our time in a state of anxiety, wondering if every little thing we wanted to do might bring the world crashing down around our ears.

Some children, unfortunately, grow up in families in which parents never teach principles and never establish clear rules or guidelines. These children usually become adults who can't function in society. Their lives reflect nothing but the chaos and uncertainty of their early lives. But this is not the way God intended families to be. And it is not the way He runs His own family.

What, then, are the eternal principles and purposes that can help us understand and apply God's will in every situation of our lives? The Scriptures give us so much guidance in this area that we could devote an entire book to that question alone. But this is a book about prayer and changing God's mind, so we'll confine ourselves to the principles that will help us decide how to know we are asking according to His will. Until we're sure about that, we can't hope to pray effectively.

Here are seven points. In the next chapter we'll apply these principles to situations you and I face every day.

Number 1: Realize that God's will is something we get to know progressively, not instantaneously.

As our intimacy with Him grows, so does our understanding of His will. We can't expect to understand everything about Him *or* His will during our lifetimes on this earth. The only man who ever knew and obeyed Him perfectly was Jesus.

But we have an eternal destiny in Jesus and (as I noted in the last chapter) we will be exploring the richness of God's character forever. Right now we simply make a beginning. We are children getting to know our Father. We try to discover as much as we can about who He is so that we can enjoy our relationship with Him and grow closer throughout the ages to come. As our prayers draw us closer to God, He shows us more and more of Himself, and His will becomes our will.

Number 2: Remember that although we can know God's will most of the time simply by knowing and obeying His Word, there will be times when we need— and can expect—specific guidance about situations where His will is unclear.

We are not slaves to the Law of God; it is our schoolmaster, the Bible says. It points us to Christ because it teaches us that we cannot obey God perfectly all the time. We're human, and we need the grace, forgiveness and guidance of God. No matter how well we get to know God, and no matter how totally we surrender our lives to Him, there will always be those occasions when we aren't sure what God wants us to do. When we face this kind of problem we have a right to clear guidance, and God will always give it.

The trouble most of us have with this, of course, is that (as I said at the beginning of this chapter) we too often say we need a word from the Lord to tell us His will when He has already revealed it. So we should make sure, before we ask for special guidance, that we don't already have it.

I heard about a married Christian man who said, "I've fallen in love with another woman, and I'm thinking of divorcing my wife to marry her. I'm praying that God will give me a sign if I'm not supposed to do it." God is not going to answer this man's prayers; His will is already clear and there's no need for a voice from heaven to confirm it. The man is merely playing games with God, hoping to use His silence on the matter as an excuse to sin.

So here's a good rule to follow: If you're asking for special guidance and are not getting it, examine what you already know of God's will to see if you don't already have your answer.

There are legitimate circumstances, however, in which we cannot discern what we should do or how we should pray, and when that happens we can ask God to give special help. He will provide reliable guidance so we can stay in the center of His will. The Holy Spirit will work in a variety of ways to show us the will of God in specific situations.

As we thoughtfully observe circumstances and events in our lives, for example, we will often get clues about what God wants us to do. A woman might contemplate making a career change that would require a move to a distant city, and as she prays for God's direction she might find that people unexpectedly cross her path to encourage and help her make the move. This could be God speaking through the circumstances to reveal His will.

But the woman should not make her decision solely on that basis. She can also ask the Holy Spirit to confirm this direction in some specific way that would remove all doubts.

God is always willing to confirm His will to us, by the way, because our asking is evidence of faith. Some have said that Gideon sinned when he put out his fleece, asking God to confirm and reconfirm His will. But God gave Gideon exactly what he asked for! There's nothing wrong with asking for this kind of help when we really need it. More about fleeces and confirmation in chapter 5.

But it's wise to be sure, when we ask God for confirmation of His specific will, that we are ready to obey Him when He does it. If we use requests for confirmation as a delaying tactic, we're out of line. And if we hope to use *lack* of confirmation as an excuse to sin, the way the man we just discussed was doing, we're in big trouble. It is as we seek to know and pray for and *do* the will of God that the Holy Spirit will direct our thoughts and actions.

Number 3: Never pray, "*If* it is Your will. . . ."

Coming at prayer like that is a sure way to destroy its effectiveness. Although many think it is a biblical pattern, it is actually an insult to God!

When we say that, God tells us, "I don't want to hear that kind of talk! Don't you know Me well enough to know My will? If you don't know Me, why should I give you anything?" But Christians have been saying this for years. Why? They have taken a single verse (James 4:15) out of context and have built it into a doctrine that fits conveniently into the Christian fatalism we discussed in the first chapter.

In this case, the verse is part of James' reproof of men

who were boasting about how successful they would be in their business schemes. James says to them, in essence, "You don't even know if you're going to be alive next year, and you're boasting about how rich you're going to be? You should be saying, 'If the Lord will, we may do this or that next year.' " These men obviously forgot Solomon's words: "Do not boast about tomorrow, for you do not know what a day may bring forth" (Proverbs 27:1).

James was criticizing those men for two reasons: First, because they were bragging about things they had no way of knowing (which was arrogant), and second, because they did not take God's will into account (which was presumptuous). God never told us to become rich or successful; in fact, He told us again and again not to get caught up in the pursuit of this world's transient pleasures and treasures. If these businessmen had known much about God, they would have had a different attitude. They would have sought humbly to do God's will instead of puffing themselves up with pride over their own foolish plans. Not that God wants us to be failures! He simply wants us to seek *Him*, not the things that moths and rust will destroy.

At any rate, James' statement is a far cry from saying that we should always pray *"If* it is Your will." This is the only verse in the Bible, in fact, that suggests that anyone should ever say, *"If* the Lord will, we will do such-and-such." The rest of the Bible tells us we can, and should, know God's will by knowing God Himself and understanding His Word. Then we can live and pray with power and authority—not for our own selfish benefit, but for God's glory.

Sometimes Christians also use the words of Jesus in the Garden of Gethsemane to bolster the idea that we should pray "If it is Your will." You'll recall that in His prayer Jesus said, "My Father, if it is possible, may this cup be taken from me. Yet not as I will, but as you will." He also prayed, "Father, if it is not possible for this cup to be taken away unless I drink it, may your will be done" (Matthew 26:39, 42)

But was Jesus *really* saying, "Father, I don't want to die on the cross—but I'll do it if You insist"? I don't believe that for a moment. Remember, it was only a short time before this that Jesus said, referring to His coming crucifixion: "What shall I say? 'Father, save me from this hour'? No, it was for this very reason I came to this hour" (John 12:27). Obviously Jesus would not make such an emphatic statement and then do a complete about-face in the Garden and ask God to keep Him from the cross.

Then what *was* Jesus praying for in the Garden? I'm convinced that the "cup" He was asking God to take from Him was *premature death in the Garden* as a result of the crushing satanic pressure that caused Him to sweat drops of blood (Luke 22:44) as His soul was "overwhelmed with sorrow to the point of death" (Matthew 26:38). Jesus knew that if He died in the Garden as a result of this pressure, His ultimate mission on earth could not be accomplished. So His prayer was, in essence, "Father, let *this* cup pass: I don't want to die here in the Garden. If You have changed Your mind about the cross, I'm asking You to change it again. And if You have changed that plan, why did You not tell me? (*That* was the greatest reason for His agony.)

You see, even Jesus prayed to change God's mind. Hebrews tells us that He was heard in this prayer (Hebrews 5:7), and we know that He not only survived the agonizing experience in the Garden, He was strengthened by it. After He finished praying, Jesus' words to His disciples were almost triumphant: "Rise, let us go! Here comes my betrayer!" (Matthew 26:46).

Jesus' prayer in the Garden, then, was hardly the fatalistic "Thy will be done" prayer most Christians believe it was. Certainly we cannot use that prayer as justification for our own apathetic or passive prayers. When Jesus ended His prayers in the Garden by saying, "Not as I will, but as you will" (Matthew 26:39), He was saying, "I am going to obey You, Father, even if My will is different from Yours." It was an affirmation of absolute commitment to the Father's purposes and will.

We must have that kind of commitment as well. We may disagree with what we perceive to be the mind of God in certain matters, and He may invite us to change His mind about those matters, but we must be willing to obey Him even if He doesn't change His mind.

Number 4: Make the salvation of others a primary prayer concern.

This is one sure way to apply God's expressed will in our prayer lives. In the third chapter of Ephesians Paul first describes the will of God for his life, which is

> to preach to the Gentiles the unsearchable riches of
> Christ, and to make plain to everyone the adminis-
> tration of this mystery [that through the Gospel the
> Gentiles are heirs together with Israel, members of
> one body and sharers in the promise in Christ Jesus],
> which for ages past was kept hidden in God, who
> created all things. Ephesians 3:8–9

After this, Paul makes one of the most profound state-
ments in the Scriptures about God's purpose and will
for His creation:

> [God's] intent was that now, through the church, the
> manifold wisdom of God should be made known to
> the rulers and authorities in the heavenly realms, ac-
> cording to his eternal purpose which he accomplished
> in Christ Jesus our Lord. In him and through faith in
> him we may approach God *with freedom and confidence.*
> Ephesians 3:10–12

Do you understand? God's expressed will and intention is that we, the Body of Christ, should demonstrate
to "rulers and authorities in the heavenly realms" the
depth and breadth of His wisdom *by our prayers.* That is
our role, individually and as a Church, and every angel,
every demon, every principality or power in the realm
of God is watching our performance. (If you have always felt like a nobody in this world, you can stop right
now!) It's time we all realized who we are as people
redeemed by Jesus Christ. The "eternal purpose" of
God is being accomplished in us through His Son.

And what *is* that eternal purpose? Here is what Jesus said:

> "I have come down from heaven not to do my will but to do the will of him who sent me. And *this is the will of him who sent me, that I shall lose none of all that he has given me, but raise them up at the last day.* For my Father's will is that everyone who looks to the Son and believes in him shall have eternal life."
>
> John 6:38–40

We must not neglect prayers for the salvation of others. Paul applied this to the prayer lives of all believers when he instructed Timothy:

> I urge. . . that requests, prayers, intercession and thanksgiving be made for everyone. . . . This is good, and pleases God our Savior, who wants all men to be saved and to come to a knowledge of the truth. For there is one God and one mediator between God and men, the man Christ Jesus, who gave himself as a ransom for all. . . . I want men everywhere to lift up holy hands in prayer.   1 Timothy 2:1, 3–6, 8

So we see here that there's one thing we can pray that will always be in the center of God's will: Whenever we pray for someone's salvation, we are asking according to His will. We can say, conversely, that it is never God's will that anyone should be lost. People can freely choose not to accept Jesus Christ, but *it is never God's will that this should happen.*

This should give us tremendous freedom and confidence in our prayers. You can pray, "God, I *know* it's Your will that my children [or parents or friend] be saved, so I'm going to ask You and keep on asking until You do it!" You *never* have to say, "God, save my children *if it is Your will.*"

I can never forget an experience I had at the Worldwide Evangelization Crusade in London. That evening I preached about radical faith, saying I believe in being an "extremist" where love is concerned. (If I'm going to be rebuked in heaven, I told them, I'd rather be rebuked for loving too much than for loving too little during my time on this earth. It has always seemed to me that we tend to be overly careful about loving wholeheartedly. Perhaps we're afraid of getting hurt by letting other people into our hearts.)

I even managed to say that if C. T. Studd, the great pioneer missionary and founder of that particular mission, were to apply for membership today, he would probably be turned down as being "too fanatical." After all, what sort of missionary would write a booklet with the provocative title D.C.D.? C. T. Studd did! He even claimed that Jesus became a D.C.D. when He hung on the cross to take our sin. He became a curse because He "Did not Care a Damn."

Anyway, at the close of that service a couple, fine young Scottish friends, stopped to talk for a few minutes, and the husband, Alistair, told me with a big grin, "Andrew, we soon expect our first baby, D.V."

"D.V.," as Alistair used that expression, meant *Deo*

volento, a Latin phrase that translates "God willing." It's an expression that's become popular among Christians in recent years. But when Alistair said that, I immediately responded, "Alistair, God *wants* you to have this baby! Don't deviate from His plan. Never say 'D.V.'— after all, you *know* His will!" And in due time, yes, Alistair and his wife had a wonderful baby.

Knowing this principle, we can also intercede for the whole world. "Father," I can say, "I know it is Your will that *all* men should be saved; therefore, I ask You to save the man I met last week in Beirut. I ask You to save the leaders of my country. I ask You to save the terrorists who are doing such terrible things out of misguided zeal for their false religion." I can pray for everyone I know, for people I have never met, for beggars on the streets of Bogota, for people in the headlines of my newspaper, for world leaders and authorities in my nation. I can, as the poet James Montgomery said, "move the arm that moves the world, and bring salvation down!"

And I can take it still further: I can pray, "Father, show me what I can do to introduce these people to You." Then I must do what He shows me. I can use my resources to go—or to send others if I cannot go—to the people who need Christ desperately. I can take Bibles to those hungry for God's Word. I can go to the suffering Church and minister the love and encouragement of Jesus wherever He is needed—in my own nation or in Eastern Europe, America, the Far East, Russia, the Middle East, Central and South America, Africa.

There are no closed doors for me. I can go because God's will is that everyone be saved, and I have a responsibility to do everything in my power to work and to pray that His will may be done. I can go with the assurance that God goes with me, because it is the expressed will of Jesus:

> "All authority in heaven and on earth has been given to me. Therefore go and make disciples of all nations . . . teaching them to obey everything I have commanded you. And surely I will be with you always, to the very end of the age."
>
> Matthew 28:18–20

The promise of Jesus is that He will be with me *as I do what He has commanded,* thus fulfilling the will of God. I cannot take "I will be with you always" as my promise, and ignore "Go." That isn't how it works. I must take the whole counsel of God, not the bits and pieces that make me feel warm and comfortable. I must meet God's conditions, and then He will fulfill His promises.

This, you see, is how we should be living. In the matters where we know God's will—as we do in most things—we should be praying for it to be done, and—to the extent that we are able—we should be doing it. The Scriptures are the foundation for all guidance and we can act upon them without doubt. God is working within us "to will and to act according to his good purpose" (Philippians 2:13). As we go about our lives we can ask, "Am I doing the will of God as He has revealed it in the Scriptures?" The answer will tell us whether or not we are on the right track.

Number 5: Look to the Holy Spirit to serve as your Guide on matters that are difficult to discern.

He speaks in a "still, small voice" within us when we open ourselves to His direction. God's Spirit is available 24 hours a day to "guide [us] into all truth" (John 16:13) whenever we seek Him. We'll talk more about this kind of guidance in just a moment.

Number 6: Obey the Ten Commandments.

This may seem obvious, but you would be surprised how many times I have heard confusion expressed concerning them.

God gave us many specific declarations of His will that we can apply to almost every situation in our lives, but the Ten Commandments God handed down to Moses on Mount Sinai leave little room for questions about God's will in vital areas: Don't murder, steal, lie or commit adultery; don't covet what belongs to others; don't use His name profanely or frivolously; keep the Sabbath holy; treat your parents honorably; and above all, don't worship anything or anyone but God. Even little children can understand such straightforward expressions of God's will.

In our prayer lives, these commandments can serve as a checklist to remove confusion we might have over whether something we're praying for is God's will or not. If you're praying for something that violates one of the commandments of God, it's safe to assume that your prayer won't be answered. I can't pray, for example, that God will protect me when I lie. When I carry Bibles across borders into nations where they are illegal, I pray beforehand that the border guards will not ask me if I have Bibles hidden in my vehicle. If they ask me, I must tell them the truth. I cannot lie to them and then say, "God, please keep me out of trouble by making them believe my lie!" God would not hear that prayer, even though His will is I should take my Bibles into that country. The will of God is also for me to tell the truth. So I pray, before I reach the border, "God, please keep the guards from asking me about Bibles." And so far, I have never been asked! God honors our prayers when we honor His will by doing it, even when it may be dangerous.

Number 7: Let love be your motivation for changing God's mind.

This is revealed in the words of Jesus. He said, for example,

> "My command is this: Love each other as I have loved you. Greater love has no one than this, that one lay down his life for his friends. You are my friends if you do what I command. . . . I chose you to go and bear fruit—fruit that will last. Then the Father will give you whatever you ask in my name."
>
> John 15:12–14, 16

Earlier in the same chapter Jesus said, "This is to my Father's glory, that you bear much fruit, showing yourselves to be my disciples" (John 15:8).

These passages tell us several important things about God's will as it relates to the kind of prayer life we are trying to develop. First, we see that the will of God is for us to love others "above and beyond the call of duty"— even to the point of laying down our lives for them. We also see that we can prove we are His friends by obeying Him and bearing fruit for the Father's glory.

That is, we show our love for Jesus by loving as He loves, through the power of His abiding presence in us. Our oneness with Him will make our lives fruitful. The Father will be honored, and our prayers will be attuned to His purposes so perfectly that whatever we ask of the Father will be given us (John 15:16).

Jesus was talking in this passage not only about the will of the Father for us and our world, but also the will of the Father for Him. Jesus never commanded us to do anything on our own. "Without Me," He said, "you can do nothing." He was sent so that all men might be reconciled to the Father, and as we become a part of His family, our love for Jesus should impel us to help Him complete this unfinished task. We are His Body, and all that He is becomes ours to the extent that we allow Him to dwell in us. This is why Paul said, "We have the mind of Christ" (1 Corinthians 2:16). Our carnal minds cannot understand anything about God, but the mind of Christ *in us*, as revealed by the Holy Spirit, guides us into all Truth.

So when we pray with the mind of Christ, we can ask God for anything, and it will be ours. When we are in that position, you see, we will be asking *only* for those things that are the perfect will of God. And if our carnal minds sometimes refuse to allow the mind of Christ to rule in our lives, the Holy Spirit will immediately remind us and draw us back to the will of the Father. As we become more and more sensitive to His leading, our actions will more perfectly reflect His will.

And when we feel gripped to pray that He will change His mind about an issue, He will hear us.

We have talked a lot about knowing God and the reasons that is so important. It is only as we know Him that we understand the unchanging and eternal purposes that govern His will for our lives. And it is within this framework that we can live boldly, as God intends.

We can act with the maturity and confidence that come from understanding what pleases God and what doesn't. We can have the security of knowing, every moment of our lives, that we are in the center of His will and that our actions fulfill His purposes. This security removes the immobilizing fears and doubts—and the excuses as well—that keep so many of us from realizing our potential as Christians.

4
Come Boldly
Before
the Throne

Often someone will say to me as we talk about changing God's mind, "But how do I know what God has decided to do in the first place? After all, He doesn't speak to me from a burning bush the way He did to Moses. And even if He did, how would I know when His plans are subject to change? I just don't see how I can make that kind of judgment."

Sometimes the most elementary questions can be the most thought-provoking. Indeed, how *can* you know what God has made up His mind to do? I will be the first one to admit there is no way I can know for sure when He has made a decision in a specific situation unless He expressly says so. Without a direct revelation—like the one Jonah received when God announced His plans to destroy Ninevah in forty days (Jonah 3:1–4)—it would seem highly presumptuous even to talk about influencing those plans, much less, as we will learn, go about doing it.

But can I expect God to reveal Himself to me the same way He did to the Old Testament prophets? There may be circumstances in which this happens today. Indeed, I have heard some remarkable stories—from countries in the Middle and Far East, particularly—where Jesus reportedly walked right into people's houses and spoke with them. In some of these appearances, witnesses described miraculous healings and even the raising of the dead.

Most of the time, however, even Christians who know God intimately don't hear from Him so directly or dramatically. I believe this is because in most situations we simply don't need that kind of experience. When I must go from Holland to America I don't need to be able to walk across the Atlantic; I can take a plane. So the Lord doesn't miraculously bid me to walk on water the way He did Peter. And I wouldn't think of asking Him for it.

But people do seem to long for dramatic supernatural experiences—not because they need them, necessarily, but often simply because they are looking for something to shore up their faith. When they get their miracles, however, they are rarely changed by them. Why? Because dramatic and unusual experiences do not constitute a relationship. One miracle, or even several, does not keep anyone in the faith. The Israelites of Moses' and Abraham's time witnessed miracle after miracle, but they became idolaters anyway.

Back in the early 1950s in my own village of St. Pancras, when our little band of believers went around telling everyone we could find about Jesus, we encountered a lot of people who said to us, "Well, if God heals that poor sick girl in your group, *then* we'll believe." Everyone knew this girl. She was terribly ill with tuberculosis. So we prayed for her and she was instantly, miraculously healed—just like that! A tremendous miracle, like something out of the New Testament. But nobody believed!

That hardly ever works, you see. And there are countless Christians who have themselves been healed, or have witnessed other spectacular miracles, but who later have fallen into unbelief. We look at that and think, "How can this be? If I experienced a miracle I could never doubt the Lord again!"

But experiences wear off. You have only to ask a wife of fifty years whether she is still married to her husband because of how charming and attentive he was on their wedding day. If their relationship has not grown since then, and if their first heady experience of high romance has not matured through years of commitment, thoughtful communication, and mutual respect and affection, then even the most ecstatic memories of her perfect bridegroom and glorious honeymoon could not keep the marriage intact.

We simply cannot survive on experiences, no matter how thrilling they may seem at the time. They're like last week's dinner—lovely at the moment, but quickly used up. If I were depending on last Wednesday's delicious chicken stew to give me energy today, I'd be in real trouble!

It is the same with God. It's not the dazzling mountaintop experiences that reveal Him to us; it is His continuous daily presence in the ordinary and extraordinary events of our lives.

One of the most intriguing titles of Oswald Chambers' many books is *Can You Come Down?* His point was that we cannot remain forever on the mountaintop the way Peter hoped to do after the transfiguration of Jesus and the appearance of Moses and Elijah (Matthew 17: 1–4). We must inevitably come down again into the valley, where the conflict of real life surrounds us. It is there that the presence of Jesus is more real than on the mountain, where we may not be able to do or say anything sensible.

As we walk with Him, we learn to know and trust His love. Over time He builds in us slowly, steadily the faith and wisdom we need to pray with all the insight, power and authority Jesus talked about.

It is incredible, really, to realize that because of what Jesus accomplished on the cross, we can relate to God on a level that the prophets who witnessed His greatest miracles could not have imagined in their wildest dreams. It is impossible to overemphasize the cosmic significance of the cross.

As a result of the sacrifice Jesus made for us, we have been restored to even more of the position Adam and Eve enjoyed before they sinned.

The devil's statement, "You will be like God, knowing good and evil" (Genesis 3:5) was deliberately deceptive, of course. He did not tell Adam and Eve that they would not have the power to do good nor would they have the power not to do evil. We, however, through the Holy Spirit, have the power to do good, which is to keep the commandments of God, and we have the power not to do evil.

We can walk and talk with the Father 24 hours a day. Nothing stands in our way. The bloody altars of sacrifice have been demolished, the Law has been fulfilled once and for all, and the "iron curtain" separating mankind from the holiest of holy places where God met only with a chosen few has been torn away forever.

When Jesus stretched out His arms and died, those were the open arms of our God welcoming us back into unhindered fellowship with Him. I like to believe it was at that moment that the angel of God was dispatched to earth with the stunning invitation that still echoes across time:

> The Spirit and the bride say, "Come!" And let him who hears say, "Come!" Whoever is thirsty, let him come; and whoever wishes, let him take the free gift of the water of life.   Revelation 22:17

Yes, because of Jesus we no longer have to guess what God is like or wonder what He wants from us. We know the Father because we have seen and known His Son. We no longer have to speculate about God's purposes or will, because Jesus has told us what they are. He has also given us His Word—the perfect mirror of His character, the master blueprint of His plans for our world. And He hasn't left us on our own to apply and interpret this vast amount of information; He has sent His Spirit to live in us, guiding us into all truth. As if this were not enough, He has also made every believer a member of the Body of Christ—the Church—and our membership in that Body adds tremendously to our understanding of God's ways with man. As we have seen, it is "together with all the saints" that we glorify Him and carry out His purposes and will in the world.

Through these means, then, God has graciously provided everything we normally need to comprehend His plans and to participate in the execution of His will through our prayers. Our intimacy with the Father through Christ, our knowledge of the Scriptures, the constant guiding presence and enlightenment of the Holy Spirit and the operation of the Spirit's gifts through the Church form an unshakable foundation for our understanding of what God is doing today.

Until we understand this, it is easy to forget that God wants to communicate with us infinitely more than we do with Him. There is no reason we should look upon His ways as "past finding out," as most Old Testament believers did. He isn't hiding or playing games. He has gone to tremendous lengths to open His mind and heart to us, and to draw us so close that we can participate in all He is doing in our world—now and throughout eternity.

The only problem (if you could call it that) is that God's accessibility has made life somewhat more complicated for those among us who still don't grasp what is involved in this kind of New Covenant relationship. Some Christians would like it a lot better, in fact, if God still spoke to us the way He did in the days of the prophets. But can they possibly imagine what our lives would be like today if He did? We would still be living under the elaborate Old Testament system of laws and ordinances, struggling to obey the commands relayed to us by God's messengers without ever knowing God personally.

Not that God ever wanted it that way. His plan was for all of us to know Him as Adam and Eve originally did. And His New Covenant with mankind through Jesus not only *restores* the possibility of that kind of intimacy; it *requires* it. Without that kind of relationship, we find ourselves in a far worse position than the Israelites of Moses' time because we can no longer rely upon prophets to act as our intermediaries. Nor can we blame them when they lead us astray. God holds us personally responsible because He has made Himself personally accessible to everyone through Jesus.

So, while it is true that life might be simpler if God still related to us as He did in Abraham's and Moses' time, He always had greater things in mind for us. Jesus told us that God has elevated us to a new position in His Kingdom. We are no longer called *servants*, because servants don't know what their master is doing. We are called *friends*, because Jesus has shared with us His full knowledge of the Father (John 15:15). God has invited us to participate in the planning and execution of His will on earth by drawing so close to Him that not only do we understand what He is doing, but we actually get involved in His decision-making processes. In other words, we become part of His plan. When this happens, we know automatically when and in which ways God is open to change.

We have been given an absolute right to this kind of guidance. If this were not so, then we would have to conclude that the Advent of Christ and His Church, the writing of the Scriptures and the arrival of the Holy Spirit in the world constituted a giant step backward for mankind. If we don't understand far *more* about God's ways than Old Testament believers did, we have missed the boat completely!

You would probably never have the nerve to call the President of the United States or of the Soviet Union (if you could reach him) to ask about some specific action he has taken: "Why did you do that? Will you listen to some of my ideas before you go any further?" But you would not hesitate to ask the same questions of a spouse or parent. Intimacy makes all the difference.

Even as we begin to develop this kind of intimacy with God, however, some of us have a problem understanding how to reach the point at which we can say, "I know God has decided to do *this,* and I'm going to ask Him to change His mind." Precisely how do we learn what God is going to do next, say, in Eastern Europe or South Africa or China or, for that matter, in our own families? And how do we know when it is appropriate to ask Him to change His plans? Perhaps it will be easier to explain if I speak from my own experience. Not that my experience is universal, but it may help illustrate the ways in which the Lord most often reveals Himself today.

Many times in my life, God has chosen to communicate with me quite directly—not what I would call miraculously, but still directly, through His Spirit. It happened once when I was smuggling a carload of several hundred Bibles into Moscow. My companion and I had parked our specially built station wagon on the street, and we were starting to unload the Bibles from their hidden compartments so we could carry them to a church. A very dangerous situation, but not an uncommon one for me.

I looked up at one point and noticed a perfectly ordinary-looking man who had stopped to watch what we were doing. This was not especially remarkable; people often watched us while we were unloading our vehicles, and we paid little attention because they were only curious. But in my heart I knew this man was different. How? I can explain it only by saying that God's Spirit disturbed something within my own spirit. It was a subtle thing.

My reaction to that inner warning was not unlike it might have been if an old friend had whispered in my ear, "Andrew, watch out!" I recognized the Holy Spirit's subtle "voice" as a result of many years of friendship with Him. This ability to "hear" the Spirit grows over time, of course. Listening is one of the most important parts of our relationship with God.

I responded almost instinctively to the warning. First, I simply prayed silently as we continued to unload the Bibles. Almost in the same moment I began to pray, the man turned and walked away quickly.

In other circumstances, I would have breathed a sigh of relief at his departure. This time, however, I said to my colleague, "That man is on his way to report us at the KGB office." There was no mistaking the urgency I felt in my spirit, and there was no doubt in my mind about what was about to happen. So we stopped unloading and prayed together, asking God to divert the man—by whatever means necessary—to give us time to unload and deliver our precious cargo. We prayed against the evil powers that threatened to keep God's Word from the people who had been waiting years to receive it. When we finished praying, we went back to our task with full assurance that God had done what we asked. The Bibles were delivered without incident.

To this day I don't know exactly what God did to keep us safe in that situation, but I am certain that unless He had revealed to me the danger we were in and unless we had prayed, we would have ended up being questioned by the KGB that day. And if we had, we might have ended up in prison.

Some Christians would argue, no doubt, that prison might have been where God wanted us, and on other occasions I would agree to that possibility. Sometimes God needs a witness in prison, so He allows Christians to be incarcerated. But that day He did not want my friend or me in prison. He wanted us to deliver our Bibles, and that is what we did. How do I know? Because He warned me of the danger. That was God's way of offering us the chance to participate in the execution of His will by asking Him to change the outcome of the situation.

We could have ignored God's warning, of course. And if we had landed in prison as a result, we could still have executed His eternal will by ministering to our fellow prisoners or to our captors. But we could not have delivered those Bibles, which in my view was God's highest and best will in that specific situation. So He warned us, expecting us to heed that warning and carry out His plans. God's will would not have been thwarted if we had failed to heed it; indeed, He would have caused all things to work together for good. But I am convinced that in this case, we were able to do that which God *most* wanted us to do—deliver our Bibles—because we understood what He was telling us and acted upon that information by praying. This kind of revelation gives us extraordinary opportunities to work hand in hand with God.

But this is by no means the only way God reveals Himself to me. It is not even the way He usually does. Ninety-five percent of the time God reveals what I need to know through far less direct means, usually through a combination of spiritual insight gained over many years of friendship with Him and what I call "circumstantial evidence." Let me give you an example of how this works.

One day in Beirut as a businessman and I walked through the bombed-out rubble where hundreds of men, women and children had died, he said to me, "Andrew, God is fed up with us! He is no more in this place. He has gone away. He has forsaken us. All you have to do is look around and you can see it."

Now someone else might have said to that man, "God has not left; He's still here!" But I didn't say that. I looked around and thought, *I must admit, I've never seen a place that looks more God-forsaken.* We were standing in a place that had once been a beautiful, thriving city. Now it was a devastated war zone. Shots rang out on the streets around us. Mutilated bodies were being carted away. Looking at all this, I understood that in this man's perception—and probably in that of most people in Beirut—God had simply decided to wash His hands of this city. And with what I have learned in the many years I have visited Lebanon, I could see how they would draw that conclusion.

So I didn't dispute my friend's remarks. Instead I said, "Yes, it sure looks that way. Maybe God *has* made up His mind to abandon Beirut. But if enough people like you repented and invited God back again, I'm sure He would change His mind!"

Now how could I make such a statement? Did God appear in my bedroom that morning and announce, "Andrew, I'm going to abandon Beirut unless they turn to Me"? Of course not. But the circumstantial evidence, combined with an understanding of that part of the world and of God's Word, character and purposes, convinced me that Beirut was probably going to be reduced to a heap of ruins very soon unless some serious repentance took place. I also knew that the Lord's will was for Beirut's inhabitants to be saved. So I could draw a conclusion: "Yes, it looks like God has made up His mind, but His mind can be changed!"

I can hear someone protesting, "But Andrew, weren't you a bit presumptuous to talk that way? Wouldn't it have been safer and more accurate to say, 'We can't be one hundred percent certain what God has decided in Beirut'?"

I don't accept that. If we had to wait until we were one hundred percent certain about *anything*, we would be paralyzed. We would never draw any conclusions and we would never know when or how to pray. For that matter, we wouldn't even be able to decide when or how to make breakfast!

And, in fact, even if God had spoken to me the way He did with Abraham before He was going to destroy Sodom and Gomorrah (Genesis 18), I still would be in the same position Abraham was in—which was a very human position, and a rather uncertain position at that. Was Abraham one hundred percent sure God would spare those wretched cities if He could find fifty (or even ten) righteous people living there? No. But he took a chance—based on his own limited human perception of what God had told him—and prayed anyway. It might have been presumptuous by some people's standards, but Abraham wasn't concerned so much about the safety of his own position as he was about the people God was about to destroy.

And God honored him because of that. He didn't say, "Abraham, where did you get the crazy idea that I would change My mind for the sake of ten righteous people? I never told you that. Shame on you!"

No, God did something else: He said yes to everything Abraham asked—not for Sodom and Gomorrah's sake, but for Abraham's. You see, the accuracy of Abraham's perception was not the issue, nor was presumption. His friendship with God was. And in this case, I am convinced Abraham didn't go far enough in "presuming" upon that friendship. Why? Because the final outcome for Sodom and Gomorrah was the same as if Abraham had not prayed at all.

The cities would have self-destructed eventually, of course, because they were rotten from the inside. But Abraham, with his limited human understanding, could not bring himself to presume that God might change His own plans of destruction for the sake of fewer than ten righteous people, and ten could not be found. Like many of us, Abraham stopped too soon in his prayers.

There is an important lesson in this. It seems to me that too many Christians today think they are in danger of offending God by presuming too much. We hear it all the time: "I can't pray for healing; that's presumptuous!" The danger in most cases is not that we might presume too much, but rather that we presume far too little; the person might die before we decide it's O.K. to pray for him! When God takes the initiative and we accept the responsibility, when our prayers stay within the boundaries of God's expressed will as we understand it, we are not being presumptuous.

While there are always ways to offend God if we set our minds to it, I think too many of us use that possibility as an excuse for not praying. It's another case in which false piety turns us into fatalists. We should make every effort to know what we are doing when we pray, naturally, but if I were sick this morning I would much rather have someone pray for me presumptuously than not pray at all! I would always prefer to be found guilty of asking too much from God than to have to admit I asked too little. And I think God would prefer it, too.

The truth is, God never told us we should not try to influence His plans until we are one hundred percent sure about what those plans are. And it's a good thing! Otherwise, places like Beirut would be wiped off the face of the earth before we could ask God to give its people one more chance to turn things around by turning to Him.

Before I visited Lebanon in July 1990, God spoke to me through the Scriptures not only about Lebanon, but also about the Middle East crisis and the return of our Lord Jesus.

> Look, their brave men cry aloud in the streets; the envoys of peace weep bitterly. The highways are deserted, no travelers are on the roads. The treaty is broken, its witnesses are despised, no one is respected. The land mourns and wastes away, Lebanon is ashamed and withers. . . . "Now I will arise," says the Lord.   NIV

I felt compelled to pass on this message to the two rival warlords in Beirut who have brought so much destruction to their nation, so I immediately began to arrange a trip to Lebanon. Not surprisingly, I encountered tremendous problems in getting a visa. Delay after delay prevented my departure until finally I appealed to the Lebanese ambassador in The Hague, who intervened personally to issue a visa without his government's formal approval.

On the night I sailed from Cyprus to Beirut, I had a terrible dream about a great calamity coming upon Lebanon: The mountains exploded, the building in which I stood trembled, the walls cracked, but personally I had deep peace. Then a voice said, "The worst for Lebanon is yet to come."

To me this was clearly the voice of God. It made me feel even more urgent about seeing the two leaders in Beirut.

When I arrived I was permitted to speak with both of these leaders. I introduced myself as a servant of God and gave both of them exactly the same message. They listened very intently. I told them, "God says: It will get much worse in Lebanon, but if *you* and your *people* will repent, then it does not have to happen. God will change His mind, because your country is so very strategic in relation to Israel, to Jerusalem, to the whole conflict in the Middle East. The whole world will watch how this conflict—which generally is perceived as a Muslim-Christian conflict—will develop in Lebanon. It is not yet too late."

Since I gave my message to those two leaders, we have seen dramatic events unfold in the Middle East.

Iraq has attacked Kuwait and has threatened to attack all countries that surround Israel. Their ultimate aim is to destroy Israel. Our hearts have been filled with anxiety as we consider the immediate future of Israel and the nations surrounding her. It certainly underlines the urgent and very practical injunction in the Scriptures to pray for the peace of Jerusalem.

If there is peace in Jerusalem, there will be peace in Baghdad, in Egypt, in Saudi Arabia, in all the border countries and ultimately in all the world. Those who have seen the utter failure of military confrontations in that part of the world know that there is no alternative but to pray—more fervently than ever—for the peace of Jerusalem. I ask you to join me as a partner in this great spiritual battle.

One of the biggest mistakes we can make is to be afraid of going too far with God. I believe it is a satanic lie that we can get away from God's will by "running ahead of the Lord" in our prayers (as I have heard well-meaning Christian teachers describe it). Naturally we should seek guidance constantly and we must do our best to move in obedience, but I believe it is actually more pleasing to God when we blunder ahead and make mistakes than when we do nothing because we are afraid.

When I still had my garden and my children were small, they would sometimes go out and pull weeds for me. I might walk into the garden an hour later and find they had pulled up most of my flowers in their efforts to do a good job! But I never scolded them. They were blameless, you see. They were learning, and as their father I knew part of the learning process was making mistakes. I didn't get angry with them because they did imperfect things out of ignorance or impetuousness. No, I loved them for wanting to please me.

God is like that with us when we pray. He understands that we are going to make mistakes, but even when we do the wrong things, He doesn't blame us.

You might argue that honest mistakes are one thing, that the Lord won't frown on us for trying, but what about when we sin deliberately, when our desires are not to please Him but to follow our own sinful or lustful or evil ways? Won't God cast us aside then?

No, and do you know why not? Because there is really no difference between small, "honest" mistakes and big, selfish ones. In the sight of God's purity they are all blunders one way or another and need forgiveness. And the person whose heart is tender toward God will find His mercy equally available.

Look at David. We know he did many wrong things, but how did God describe him? He called him "David, who kept my commands and followed me with all his heart, doing only what was right in my eyes" (1 Kings 14:8). David sinned, both innocently and deliberately, but at the base of his character was a desire to love and honor God. His relationship with God was so intimate that the moment he sinned he had to say he was sorry. Relationship is the important thing.

Or look at good old Abraham, who stumbled, lied, cheated—but when God wrote Abraham's biography in

Romans He said, "Abraham believed God" (Romans 4:3). We might say, "But he lied, he cheated!" God didn't see him that way. He said, "Abraham believed God"—period. Everything else was incidental to that. He was blameless, not perfect. There's a big difference.

We are like that when we stand before God in prayer—blameless, not perfect—and it's a wonderful position to be in. We don't have to be afraid of going too far with God. Even if we do, He won't hold it against us. His grace is bigger than our foolish mistakes.

So God doesn't expect us to wait until we have all the facts before we pray, because we can never know everything about His plans. What we *can* do is seek earnestly to know Him, study the circumstantial evidence, listen to the Holy Spirit's guidance, take our knowledge of His character into account, draw reasonable conclusions and pray accordingly. As we do that, God will teach us to make fewer mistakes and our prayers will become more and more effective. We may often hear and understand Him imperfectly, but He will continue His promised work of perfecting us as we draw closer to Him.

All of this may be more complex for us than the miraculous revelations of Old Testament times, but it's also far more instructive. God is teaching us in practical ways, often through trial and error, how to apply the knowledge He has given us.

There can be no sin, then, in asking the Lord for whatever we believe will accomplish His will and purposes, regardless of our insecurity about our own limitations. We don't have to know the full scope of His plans to conclude that they are subject to change. God is always happy to hear our requests, even when our understanding is extremely limited, as Abraham's was when he interceded for Sodom and Gomorrah.

"You may ask me for anything in my name," Jesus said, "and I will do it" (John 14:14). I think those words are the ultimate answer to all our questions about when and how we can ask God to change His mind. Not that we should ask foolishly or recklessly or out of ignorance. But if we do, God will forgive us and use our mistakes to make us wiser the next time. The only people who don't make mistakes are the ones who never do anything for God or ask anything from Him—and if we should worry about anything, that's it!

5
How, Then,
Shall We Pray?

Now that we have a clearer picture of what it takes to come before God's throne and ask Him to change His plans, it is time to look more specifically at how we can go about doing it. We have already uncovered, in the stories of Moses, Elijah and other prophets mentioned in previous chapters, some vital clues about how these legendary characters communicated with God and succeeded in changing His mind. We have learned some of the principles that guided their relationships with Him, principles that caused history to be rewritten as a result of their prayers.

The most important principle, as we have seen, is a recurring theme for this book. Let me say it one more time: It is only to the extent that we know God and understand His conditions for change that we are given opportunities to influence His plans. In other words, God changes His mind only for His friends—not for strangers or casual acquaintances. As we begin to look at how to pray—and in the final chapter, what we should be praying for—it's vital to remember this.

As soon as I begin to speak about how to pray in order to change God's mind, someone will usually shake his head at me and say, in the same tone of voice he would use with a naughty child, "Now, Brother Andrew, I know you don't mean to give people the impression that Christians can tell God what to do. After all, I'm sure that's not the way you pray. . . ."

This is a back door way of telling me that unless I take a fatalistic, *laissez-faire* approach to prayer, I'm a blasphemer. Such people hope that I will reply with a look of embarrassed horror, "No, no, of *course* I don't tell God what to do!" But I would never say that, because it's not true. I tell God what to do almost every time I pray!

Before you get too upset with me, let me give you an example of what I mean. Some of my most precious memories of Corrie ten Boom are of the many times we prayed together. Corrie was a passionate intercessor, and her urgency and excitement were quite infectious. You couldn't pray with her without being changed by the experience.

"Lord," she would say—except she always pronounced it "Lort," like a good Dutchwoman—"Lort, You must *do* something! There's no time to waste!" And then she would tell the Lord very specifically and very straightforwardly what she wanted Him to do. She spoke just the way she spoke to me, her old friend. Sometimes she would weep or laugh, sometimes she would argue her points quite fiercely, but always she was herself—and always she was totally honest. She held nothing back from God, and He seemed to hold nothing back from her.

Many times, in the midst of these lively prayer sessions of ours, she would quote God's own Word back to Him to remind Him of His promises. She would have made a great lawyer. When she grew especially impassioned, she would grab her Bible and thumb through the pages rapidly until she found the exact passage she could use to prove her case. Then she would lift her Bible into the air, point to the verse and say triumphantly, "Here, Lort—read it Yourself!"

I always loved that. And I'm sure God did, too. He loves it when we know Him well enough to talk to Him that way. I don't know of anybody's prayers that had more influence with God than Corrie's. She was not deterred by false piety or legalism or a need to be anyone but herself. And after all, as she would often remind Him, she was not asking God for anything He had not already promised. So she never hesitated to tell Him what to do and to thank Him when He did it. "I *knew* You would do it!" she would say with a jubilant smile. "I just *knew* it!"

And she did, you see. She knew what God would do for her because she knew God. She understood His will and expected Him to keep His Word. It never crossed her mind that He wouldn't. What faith! If only the Lord had a few more friends like Corrie, our poor old world would not be in the mess it's in today.

Now you tell me: Were Corrie's prayers blasphemous? Presumptuous? Some might say so, but I would not, because her approach was totally scriptural. Jesus said, "Ask Me for anything," and Corrie took Him up on it, always basing her prayers on her deep understanding of God's will. And God answered her prayers. How could He do otherwise?

So as we look at the question "How do we pray to change God's mind?" I begin with the little reminder that we don't pray out of a desire to change His mind or to "tell Him what to do"; our desire is to know Him better as our Friend and Father. Opportunities to change God's mind are only one result of that relationship.

With that in mind, let's talk about how we can most effectively pray when we have decided it's time to ask the Lord to change His mind about a specific situation. I would like to keep things simple, and offer just two lessons God has taught me over the years as I have tried to learn how to intercede more effectively. I have chosen to concentrate on these lessons in particular because they solve for me the problems that seem most common to Christians wherever I travel.

The Power of Focused Prayer

The first of these lessons, which I learned early in my Christian experience, taught me why some prayers are more powerful than others.

We were in a prayer meeting—it was in 1950—in our little village of St. Pancras in Holland. We were a very dedicated and energetic bunch of intercessors, and we had spent quite a long time that night praying for missions and missionaries around the world. We interceded for the millions living in every nation from China to the Congo, prayed for governments and rulers, prayed for God to do tremendous things. We believed, as I still do, that we should be praying for big things—for the souls of men and the destiny of nations—not for a better refrigerator or a nicer car. We had great faith, so we were praying boldly that night about matters of vast consequence.

Now there were in our group some relatives of a little girl named Reina, whose Christian parents had died from a tragic domestic accident only a short time before. When her parents died, Reina had gone to live with her unbelieving grandmother. Her relatives°were deeply concerned about her, so when we finished praying for world missions, we agreed to pray for little Reina. Almost as soon as we began to pray for her, the most amazing thing happened: Everyone began to cry. All of us were suddenly on our knees beseeching the Lord from the depths of our souls to intervene in that little girl's life. As we prayed, we were stirred in a way we had not been all night, and our faith multiplied as we prayed.

When we finally finished, while we were still wiping away our tears, I stood up and said to the group, "Wait a minute! What's happened here? Now we're praying for one little girl and we cry, but when we prayed for a million lost souls, we didn't cry. Why?" There was silence for a while, then someone answered, *"Because we cannot identify with the millions, but we can identify with that one."*

We went away from that meeting feeling that God had put a key into our hands. We understood something then that we had never really thought about before: We can pray for the world, for the hungry, for the oppressed, for the missionaries out on the field, for the poor, but until we can identify with and focus our prayers on one person we know about, our prayers will probably not be passionate.

After that night I understood why "God, protect the missionaries" and "God, help the people of Russia" aren't powerful prayers even though they might be big prayers and full of faith. Unless I can focus on that one missionary in prison in China, that one being persecuted in Lebanon, that one being held hostage in Colombia, unless I identify with him and understand his plight, I cannot really pray for him as I want to. But when I have taken the time to find out what he is facing, when I have experienced his discouragement over working for years without seeing a single soul won over to Christ, when I know the conditions he is living under—the torture he has suffered in captivity, the poverty and isolation and sickness he has endured, the opposition from every side—then I can pray! Then I can intercede passionately on behalf of that one missionary, or any believer.

In the years since that prayer meeting in St. Pancras, I have also made a commitment to go, wherever and whenever I can, to be with those who are the focus of my prayers, people who are cut off and struggling to survive in the most restricted and dangerous nations on earth. That's what God has called me to do. It is where I am really needed, and where I have told God I will be, because there is nobody to take my place if I don't go. I have often said to the Lord, "I don't know why it has to be me. I'm the least qualified guy You could find!" I know there are thousands of people who could be doing what I do, and probably doing it much better. But the fact is, most of them aren't doing it. So there is a tremendous void and God has to settle for me. I do all I can, but I'm only one man, and Open Doors is only one organization. Needs are not being met. The suffering Church continues to suffer.

You see, God doesn't have stand-ins. We're not replaceable. My heart breaks when I see the staggering needs in countries where nobody is taking the Word of God, or even a simple word of encouragement. I ask, "Lord, where are the people You've called to be here?"

That is one reason I preach, even though I am not

much of a preacher, and that is why I write, even though I am not a writer. I do it because I want desperately to shake you out of your lethargy if you are one of those God has called to *go,* and you have said, "No, I can't go. I have other priorities. I have my business to run, I have my responsibilities at home. God can find somebody else." He can't. You are free to choose your priorities, but if you don't do the job God has called you to do, it will go undone because nobody is waiting in the wings to do it.

It is exactly the same with our prayers: If we don't learn to focus our prayers and ask God to save our kids, our neighbors, our bosses and co-workers, our nation and the world, if we don't intercede for that poor widow we know about in some forgotten village in a remote part of the globe—then *there's nobody else to do it.* Jesus won't do it. He is not praying for the world; He's praying for *us,* so that *we* will do what He has commanded (John 17:9). It's *our* job to pray for and go into all the world (Mark 16:15).

So when you decide you are going to ask God for big things—as I hope you will—don't be satisfied to pray, "Lord, bless those nations and save those people." Pray for them specifically. Then go to them if you can. Ask God to help you make personal contacts with a few key individuals there. Get to know them. Listen to the cries of their hearts. Give them God's Word, encourage and pray with them. Do something practical to help them. If it is impossible for you to go, then study their culture, their history, their political structure, their leaders, and learn something about the forces that affect their lives, so you can pray with more insight and intelligence. I guarantee it will make all the difference in your prayers.

And you had better watch out when you begin to pray this way! The moment you say, "Lord, be with the suffering Christians in that city; give them Bibles, give them encouragement, show them that You care," God may very well reply, "Ah, that's what I've been trying to tell *you* all along!"

I heard a story recently about an American mother who learned this lesson only after several years of discouraging, unfocused prayer for the Far East. Her prayers—and her life—were transformed one day in the early 1970s when a friend handed her a news magazine that carried a photograph of an unidentified young Vietnamese mother, sobbing as she clutched a tiny mutilated body to her bosom. Her baby had been killed by bombs that had destroyed her whole village. The photograph was heart-wrenching to this American woman because as a mother, she could identify with that other young mother's agony and loss.

She was so moved by the photograph that she tore it out and taped it to the inside cover of her Bible. Starting that day, instead of praying vaguely for "the Far East" as she usually did, she looked into the face of that weeping mother and prayed for her and her whole family as well as the other suffering mothers and children in her village. After a few days of this she went to the library and came home with books and maps that gave her vivid mental images of that part of Vietnam. She began to ask the Holy Spirit to guide her prayers, and the focus of her prayers became clearer and clearer. She joined with other mothers to pray for an end to the conflict.

When the war finally ended, she came across a newspaper article about Vietnamese refugees living in a nearby community, and she made contact with one family through a social service agency. Within a year she was helping refugees in her area find employment and housing. Many of them became Christians.

In the years since then, I am told, this woman has expanded her "prayer war" for Vietnam. Today she has been joined by a large and committed circle of Christian friends who have caught her vision and are working to minister the love of Jesus to these beleaguered people. She and other members of her church adopted a number of unwanted orphans and found homes for many others who are illegitimate offspring of American servicemen. They have also helped found several new churches in Vietnam and in the U.S.

I don't know this woman's name, but that's not really important. She could be any one of us. In the moment she first identified herself with one young Vietnamese mother—instead of the whole Far East—she became a true intercessor whose prayers had a global impact. *She prayed for big things in a focused, specific way,* and eventually changed the lives of a substantial number of people who were once without hope.

Your prayers—and your obedience to the Holy Spirit's direction—can do the same. Or perhaps even more! There are no limits with God.

When God Is Silent

The second lesson is one that taught me several important things about those times when we pray with great faith and power, and we are sure we are praying according to God's will and meeting His conditions, but He doesn't seem to be answering. We have done everything "right," but He is either saying no, or is "giving us the silent treatment," as one of my friends likes to call it.

We have all experienced this problem. We pray for the healing of a devout brother or sister who is dying of some painful disease. We anoint them, we hold prayer meetings with the church, we know God is going to heal this person, but he or she doesn't get better. Or we pray for the conversion of a rebellious teenager, one who was dedicated to the Lord as a baby and has been raised by loving Christian parents, but who has become a drug addict who steals from his parents and lives a life of gross immorality. We pray and pray, but things seem to be going from bad to worse.

What do we do? How do we handle this? Amazingly enough, many Christians don't do anything. They don't respond at all! Or worse, they consign the whole experience to the convenient catch-all file labeled "Tests of Faith." They seem to take the attitude of Ali Khamenei, the leader of Iran's Muslims, who told the grief-stricken families of some 40,000 people who died in the great earthquake in June 1990 to accept the disaster as a "divine test" they must pass "through patience and cooperation." Incredible!

But the sad truth is, Christians talk like this all the time. Why? It's partly, of course, because fatalism has permeated much of our thinking, but I think there's another problem as well. We simply don't know how to respond to God's silence, so we do what seems safest and easiest: We gloss over the problem, tell ourselves that things aren't what they seem, that God has His mysterious reasons and that "someday we'll understand"—meaning someday in heaven, not in this lifetime.

We are a lot like the people in the old fable about the emperor's new clothes. They all knew something was wrong, that the emperor was parading around stark naked, but nobody was willing to be the one to point it out for fear of being thrown into the dungeon. So they all said how beautiful the emperor's new clothes were— and in pretending they eventually began to believe it themselves.

When we do this with God it isn't funny. It's tragic, because by ignoring God's silence or pretending nothing is wrong, we miss a tremendous opportunity to become more intimate with Him and find out some extremely important things about His character. We are so intent on avoiding the obvious that we miss the chance to find out the truth.

Or is it that we don't really believe God will give us our answers? Or are we afraid—afraid to take off our masks and be honest and authentic with each other and with God, and afraid of what we might discover if we do? We must not settle for that kind of "pretend" relationship with God—or with our fellow believers, for that matter. Or with a world that is looking to us for answers.

So what *should* we do when God is silent? First, I think we must go to God and *ask Him why*. That's the obvious question, isn't it? "Why did this happen? What's wrong here? Father, why aren't You healing this person? Why aren't You bringing that teenager to repentance? Why aren't You answering?" David asked the same question: "My God, my God, why have you forsaken me? Why are you so far from saving me?" (Psalm 22:1). Should I say here that even Jesus asked this question?

It's perfectly normal to ask why when we don't understand what's happening. What would you do if you called your best friend and said, "I'm sick in bed, I need you to bring me medicine," and she said, "I'll be right there," but ten hours later she still hadn't arrived? I hope you wouldn't lie there in bed saying, "This must be a test. I'm not going to ask her why she didn't come, I'm just going to grin and bear it. And anyway, she probably knows better than I do whether or not I need medicine."

Is that what you would do? Or would you call her

again and say, "Why haven't you come? You promised! What happened?" Friends don't think twice about asking each other such questions. So why shouldn't we ask God—especially when the issues and needs are vastly more important?

We have to find out the reasons. We are His friends, His children, His Body, the people for whom He died! We can't afford to make pious excuses or pretend everything is all right when it isn't. The Lord expects us to ask. "Call to me," He says, "and I will answer you and tell you great and unsearchable things you do not know" (Jeremiah 33:3).

If I have a pain in my back that is preventing me from doing work for God, and my wife and I have been praying for my healing for six weeks, it does me no good if she says, "Andrew, in God's timing you will surely be healed." That wouldn't satisfy me. That could mean six years from now! I wouldn't accept it, because I know God. I know I can go to Him directly and say, "Lord, why don't You heal me?" He's my Friend and my Father, and He knows the answer, so it would be crazy not to ask Him! What could be more logical or natural?

And I am sure, I am absolutely, positively *sure* God would find a way to give me an explanation. Maybe I wouldn't be healed—that's possible for any one of several reasons I could list—but I would have my explanation. The Holy Spirit would help me see my situation from His perspective, which would be even better than being healed; I would have gotten closer to God's heart in the process of finding out why I wasn't healed. And I would rather get closer to God than be healed any day, so I'd have nothing to lose. In any event, there has never been a case where God has failed to explain His silence when I have asked Him. There have been questions I have had to leave open for a while, but God always answers eventually if we really want to know.

Just recently He gave me the answer to a question I left open many years ago. A number of our teams were caught in East Germany over the years with the Russian Bibles they were trying to take over the borders. We lost many Bibles that way, and this troubled me. I asked God, "Are we doing something wrong? Why did You allow this? It's such a waste—all those Bibles that nobody will ever read! This cannot be Your will!" I asked and asked and never got a clear answer. So I left it open. I said, "O.K., Lord, but I expect an answer. I'll wait, but I'm not closing the file." (I never close a file without an answer!)

Then, only a few months after the Berlin Wall fell in 1989, I opened my Dutch newspaper one morning to read that the Stasi—the East German secret police—had been storing all the Russian Bibles they had taken from us, and had just shipped them off to the Church in Russia. There were *twenty thousand Bibles!* Not one was wasted, you see. I could finally close that file because I had my answer, right there in black and white: Those

Bibles were not lost; they were just "delayed in transit," and they are finally where they belong.

There is a second thing I believe we must do when God seems silent. It applies to intercession generally as well. Winston Churchill said it perfectly in his famous eight-word speech at a graduation ceremony during World War II: "Never, never, never, never, never . . . *never* give up!"

More and more these days I hear Christians say things like, "I don't pray for things more than once; I believe God heard me the first time." Some preacher made the statement—perhaps about justification—"God said it, I believe it, that settles it!" and Christians have taken that out of context and twisted it to mean something that preacher probably never intended. They say, "God said He would save my kids, I have asked Him, that settles it. Period." They convince themselves that asking again is evidence of a lack of faith—not "great faith," as Jesus said—and on that basis they stop praying.

But I believe we cannot call ourselves intercessors un- less we are willing to persist in our prayers. We must keep on praying until God moves. If my kids were not saved I would nag God night and day; I would make His life miserable until I saw every last one of them saved and walking with Him! I wouldn't take any chances. I wouldn't sit back and say, "O.K., God, I've asked, that's it!" When I am asking God for something that important—and everything I pray for is important to me—I don't quit until I know He has done it.

Sometimes I don't have to see it to know it—as, for

example, I didn't have to see it to be sure God had stopped that man in Moscow who was going to report us to the KGB. But as a general rule, I pray until I am sure.

There is a tremendous amount of Scripture to support this idea of persistence. You can start with Abraham again and his prayers for Sodom and Gomorrah. We have already recalled how he went back again and again and again, until he was finally afraid to go back and ask God one more time, and as a result he lost what he had gained (Genesis 18:23–32). This is a perfect example of what happens when we stop praying too soon!

Then there was Jacob, who wrestled with God (Genesis 32:24–29). Where are the people who will wrestle with God today, men and women who will say, "God, I won't let You go until You give me what I ask"?

The psalmist cried to the Lord "day and night" (Psalm 88:1), and so did most of the prophets of the Old Testament. God always interpreted their "much asking" as evidence of faith. And in the Gospels we have many wonderful illustrations. Those familiar to most of us are the story of the Gentile woman whose daughter was demon-possessed (Matthew 15:22–28 and Mark 7:25–30); Jesus' parable about the unjust judge (Luke 18:1–8); the incident involving the two blind men of Jericho (Matthew 20:30–34); and Jesus' story about the friend asking for bread (Luke 11:5–10).

This last illustration is a particular favorite of mine because it is the Lord's direct response to His disciples' request "Teach us to pray." Jesus first gave them the pattern of the Lord's Prayer, and immediately followed that with His parable:

> "Suppose one of you has a friend, and he goes to him at midnight and says, 'Friend, lend me three loaves of bread, because a friend of mine on a journey has come to me, and I have nothing to set before him.'
>
> "Then the one inside answers, 'Don't bother me. The door is already locked, and my children are with me in bed. I can't get up and give you anything.' I tell you, though he will not get up and give him the bread because he is his friend, yet because of the man's persistence he will get up and give him as much as he needs.
>
> "So I say to you: Ask and it will be given to you; seek and you will find; knock and the door will be opened to you. For everyone who asks receives; he who seeks finds; and to him who knocks, the door will be opened."   Luke 11:5–10

I like the Williams translation of this last verse, which is true to the spirit of the original text: "Keep on asking. . . keep on seeking. . . keep on knocking."

What a tremendous passage of Scripture! It is the same teaching as in the other passages I just mentioned and, taken together, they all convey the same message: If you really want to change God's mind, don't give up! Keep asking!

Now there are a couple of other points I would like to mention briefly in connection with what to do when God is silent. We could call them the two Fs.

Fasting and Fleeces

Whenever I finish a message on intercession, someone will stop me afterward and ask, "But Andrew, what
about fasting?" They ask this because I don't usually
talk about fasting at all.

First of all, let me make it clear that I am not against
fasting. I have fasted a lot in my life, but I don't do it as
much as I used to. Most of us eat too much anyway and
the Bible says plenty against gluttony, so fasting can be
wholesome from that standpoint alone. Some people
fast one or two days a month and give the money they
save to the poor or to the suffering Church, and I ap-
plaud that.

But I don't think Christians should use fasting as a
means of getting God's ear when He seems silent. This
is a personal opinion, you understand; it is a matter
open to argument because the Scriptures don't give us
a lot of instruction about fasting. But I personally feel
that when we come up with the idea of fasting in order
to get God's attention, it's a little like a child who holds
his breath until he turns blue—and it usually accom-
plishes just about as much. It becomes another legalistic
exercise, another way to earn merit badges to prove
how spiritual and self-disciplined we are. Carried to an
extreme, it can even become a way of trying to replicate
or add to the sacrifice of Christ.

God will not respond to that. He hears us on the basis
of what Jesus accomplished on the cross, not on the

basis of our sacrifices. I always shudder when someone tells me, "I've decided to fast forty days the way Jesus did." What's the next step, I wonder? Are they going to have someone nail them to a cross? We must be careful when we start thinking our actions give us the "right" to approach God. We can come before Him on no basis other than the sacrifice of Jesus.

But don't misunderstand me. I believe there *are* times when fasting is appropriate. Jesus said something I have adopted as my own guideline about fasting. When people asked Him why His disciples didn't fast as the Pharisees and John's disciples did, Jesus said, "How can the guests of the bridegroom fast while he is with them? They cannot, so long as they have him with them. But the time will come when the bridegroom will be taken from them, and on that day they will fast" (Mark 2:19–20).

I take from that Scripture a general principle that goes something like this: "When you are close to God and everything is going fine, you don't fast—you feast! But when you are away from God, you fast." I don't mean when you are away from God through sin, because then you wouldn't even think of it. I mean when you are away from God in the sense that you have a problem, a burden, a vision, a project, a goal, something you must master, some area in which you cannot discern the will of God or cannot understand what it is He is trying to tell you, or something you must do that you feel too far from God to accomplish. *Then* you can fast on a meaningful level.

I have fasted in those sorts of situations, and many times it has been very helpful. But again, we are talking about fasting within our intimate relationship with God through Christ. We don't *have* to fast, ever, as a way of "paying the price" for what we want. Jesus has already paid the price in full. So our fasts are for our benefit, to bring us in line with God's thinking and help us clear away the debris in our own lives. In that sense, they can have a place in any Christian's life.

There is also a place for fasting in spiritual warfare, as we'll see in the next chapter.

Now as to the matter of fleeces. The concept of fleeces comes, of course, from the story of Gideon (Judges 6:12–40). I love this story because it not only illustrates an important point about how to pray, but underlines the concepts we dealt with earlier in this chapter about asking God why.

You will probably recall that God visited Gideon to announce that He was going to use him to rescue Israel after they had been oppressed and impoverished by the Midianites and the Amalekites for seven long years. The Lord began His dialogue with Gideon by saying, "The Lord is with you, mighty warrior." What a statement! You might expect Gideon to reply, "Wow, You have a pretty high opinion of me!" But Gideon answered instead, "If the Lord is with us, why has all this happened to us? Where are all the wonders that our fathers told us about?"

Those were good questions! Gideon didn't easily accept what the Lord was telling him, because he had good reason to be skeptical. He had been through seven terrible years, and he was not about to listen to any prophecy unless he could be absolutely sure it was God speaking to him. And as his conversation with the Lord continued, his skepticism did not diminish, even when God told him, "I will be with you, and you will strike down the Midianites as if they were but one man." Gideon replied, "If I have found favor in Your eyes, give me a sign that it is really You talking to me." Then he brought an offering before the Lord, and God gave Gideon his sign by causing fire to come out of a rock and consume it.

But this wasn't enough for Gideon. Even though he realized by now that it was God he was dealing with, he wanted another sign, just to be sure he had heard right about the way God was going to use him. So he said, "If You will save Israel by my hand as You have promised— look, I will place a wool fleece on the threshing floor. If there is dew only on the fleece and all the ground is dry, then I will know that You will save Israel by my hand." A tough test, but God did what he asked.

That still wasn't enough for Gideon. He went back to the Lord and said this time he wanted the fleece dry and the ground wet. And God did that, too. After this Gideon believed what God told him and went on to defeat the enemy as God had promised.

So here we are faced with the question that is debated so hotly in many Christian circles: Was Gideon wrong to "test" God? Many Christians have condemned his attitude. "God had spoken," they say. "Gideon was wrong to question Him, and even more wrong to test Him by demanding three signs. He should have believed God the first time He spoke!"

I don't agree. I think God understood Gideon's need for confirmation and loved his attitude. There is certainly not a single indication in the Scriptures that God was offended by it. When Gideon said, "If You're with us, why has all this happened?" God's reaction was, in essence, "Gideon, you are My man!" I believe God expected Gideon to be skeptical, because he had every reason to be. And He was fully prepared to meet that skepticism with whatever confirmations Gideon wanted.

There is no end to God's patience when we ask Him to confirm His Word in our lives. That's not unbelief, that's faith! As Christians we can ask for big things, but we are usually afraid to ask even for small things. Gideon was not. He had boldness and guts. He was a true warrior! And God gave him what he needed to accomplish His will.

So I think there are times when we can put out a fleece—not on an everyday basis, nor out of a desire for dramatic experiences, but in situations like the one Gideon faced, in which God seems to be saying something quite unbelievable to us and we need a definite confirmation. There are a number of instances like this in Scripture, including God's sign to Abraham (Genesis 15:7–17) when he needed reassurance that God would give him the inheritance He promised, and to Moses (Exodus 4:1–9) when he needed proof that he had spoken with God.

These were exceptional situations, yes. But God is open to our needs, and in exceptional situations He is always doing exceptional things. So we can't let fear or false piety paralyze or deter us from doing what He has told us to do. We know how to pray: with focused, persistent prayers. We can afford to be bold. God is bigger than we can possibly imagine!

6
When It's Satan's Will, Not God's

My English stepfather, Uncle Hoppy, never asked me, "Andrew, what's the time?" Instead he asked, "Andrew, how's the enemy?"

Uncle Hoppy was always fighting the devil, always looking for new ways to outwit him or foil his plans. He understood a lot about spiritual warfare and he knew the value of constant vigilance. I admired his fighting spirit and I've tried to develop more of it myself.

Now what does spiritual warfare have to do with a book on changing God's mind? Everything. In the first place, many Christians mistake the tragedy or evil they see around them as having arisen from a loving, permissive God, when it is really the work of the enemy.

In the second place, until you try to change God's mind you will never understand spiritual warfare. The devil will oppose you on this as on nothing else because he wants evil to exist in the world.

Look at it this way: If something exists, God has not decided to abolish it. And if we ask God to change His mind about letting an evil situation or circumstance exist, Satan will do everything he can to hinder us. He wants people to live in darkness and sin and is a dedicated enemy of prayer.

So it's odd to me that many Christians today still seem almost unaware of the enemy's presence in our world, much less the fact that he doesn't want us tampering with his schemes. Even with the tremendous popularity of recent bestselling books that talk in vivid terms about battle between the forces of God and Satan, in many churches I visit there is a startling lack of knowledge about spiritual warfare. Oddly enough, this is particularly true in nations where the Gospel is preached without restriction. As I visit churches in the free world I often hear remarks like, "I don't believe in talking about the devil; I'd much rather talk about God," as if somehow we're thinking negatively when we mention Satan, and the best thing we can do is ignore him the way we might ignore a snarling dog in the hope that he'll lose interest and go away.

The suffering Church worldwide doesn't have this attitude. They've experienced firsthand what happens when you ignore the devil and expect him to extend the same courtesy. It's always possible, of course, to focus to an unhealthy degree on Satan—and he probably gets blamed for too much in some circles—but most Christians I meet don't make that mistake. They choose, for one reason or another, not to pay any attention to him at all. As a result, they are unprepared for the kind of warfare the enemy is waging today.

Some believers miss the opportunity to change God's mind because they don't believe it ever needs changing. They don't see the importance of our prayers in battling evil. They are ignorant of Satan's activities because they have misinterpreted Scriptures or taken one or two verses out of context to support their head-in-the-sand attitude. "Jesus defeated the devil on behalf of everyone who believes," they'll say, "so Satan can't touch me. I belong to God, and He controls *everything* that happens to me—including the things that may *seem* evil from a human viewpoint. I'm not going to fight those, because I'll only be fighting God's will."

This attitude shocks and dismays me for three important reasons.

First of all, it's based on a lie: that Satan is not really a threat to Christians. The Bible teaches just the opposite. Jesus warned His followers about the satanic opposition they would encounter as they preached the Gospel, portraying the devil as a murderer and "the father of lies" (John 8:44). When Satan bragged that he controlled "all the kingdoms of the world and their splendor" and had the power to give them to whomever he chose, Jesus did not dispute his claim (Matthew 4:8). He even called him "the prince of this world" (John 14:30).

113

New Testament writers identify Satan as a relentless accuser of Christians (Revelation 12:10), a tempter (1 Thessalonians 3:5), a hinderer (1 Thessalonians 2:18), "the god of this age" (2 Corinthians 4:4), "the ruler of the kingdom of the air, the spirit who is now at work in those who are disobedient" (Ephesians 2:2), the evil one (Matthew 13:19) and the enemy (Matthew 13:39). Paul warns that Satan "masquerades as an angel of light" and his servants "as servants of righteousness" (2 Corinthians 11:14–15). Peter characterizes him as "a roaring lion" hunting for a good meal and instructs us to be alert because our adversary is constantly afflicting us and our brothers and sisters all over the world (1 Peter 5:8–9).

In the face of all this, how could any Christian believe Satan is not a threat to us today?

The second thing I object to in this attitude is that it is extremely callous. Taken to its logical conclusion it says, "I'm safe and my loved ones are protected, so who cares what happens to everyone else?" Do you see what happens when you believe a lie? You start with a false premise—that Satan cannot hurt Christians—and then you are drawn into sin. In this case, the sin is one of selfishness and hardheartedness toward the rest of the world. We cannot know and love God and then turn our backs on the perishing people He has commanded us to love and rescue. Unless, of course, we believe Satan's lie. Then—as Satan well knows—anything is possible!

The third reason I'm upset about this attitude is that

it says we should not actively resist evil because it may be good in disguise. This is simply a modern rendition of the so-called "wise counsel of Gamaliel," which was about as fatalistic and *un*wise as counsel can get.

You'll recall that Gamaliel, a leader of the Pharisees, argued that the Sanhedrin should not oppose the preaching of Peter and the other apostles because "if their purpose or activity is of human origin, it will fail. But if it is from God, you will not be able to stop these men; you will only find yourselves fighting against God" (Acts 5:38–39).

As Christians we should know better than embrace that kind of faulty reasoning. We who know God have been promised all the wisdom necessary to discern the difference between what is of human origin (the flesh) and what is from God (James 1:5; 1 John 4:1–6). We don't have to resort to pious-sounding excuses for ignorance of God's purposes by saying that "cream will rise to the top"—which, in essence, is what Gamaliel did with the Sanhedrin. It was the fatalism inherent in his argument, of course, that appealed to the hypocritical Pharisees, so in that case the devil shrewdly orchestrated his own defeat. The apostles survived to preach again!

But we cannot count on that in every case. We must understand that Satan will always attempt to inject some form of anesthetic to render the Body of Christ unconscious of his presence before he attacks. Apathetic fatalism is only one of the anesthetics or devices he likes to use. We'll talk about others later in this chapter.

I'm convinced that Uncle Hoppy's question—"How is the enemy?"—is a good one for all of us to ask, because we must stay alert to what our adversary is doing. But there are two larger questions we must also answer if we're going to become the powerful intercessors God wants us to be: Who is the enemy and how can we beat him? Let's look in this chapter at exactly who Satan is, and what some of his most successful tactics are. Then, in the next chapter, we'll talk about the specific weapons and strategies we can use to defeat him.

When you see his name—Satan, the devil, Beelzebub, Lucifer—what picture comes into your mind? The cartoon character with the mischievous grin, funny horns and long, pointy tail who dresses in red underwear and carries a pitchfork? Satan loves that image, I'm sure! After all, who could take such a ridiculous figure seriously? No doubt he smirks when people buy T-shirts for their children like the ones described to me recently, which feature creative caricatures of horned scamps beneath the logos *Little Devil* and *Cute As the Devil* and—most amazing of all—*Daddy's Little Demon*.

Many Christians have trouble thinking of the devil even in these cute comic-strip terms. They can identify him only as a "negative force" or an "evil influence"—not as a real being. The devil does everything he can to foster that kind of vagueness about his identity, because he knows that the moment we see exactly who he is, we become a real threat to him. Once we see him as someone who operates in predictable ways within specific boundaries, we can anticipate his strategies, see through his disguise and combat him successfully using the powerful weapons God has provided. So the devil spends a lot of time and energy trying to keep us blind to his actual identity.

There are several descriptions of Satan in the Scriptures that can help us get a realistic picture of his character and personality. We know that Satan was originally named Lucifer, and that he belonged to an elite corps of God's angels who were given the same privilege we have been given: They could choose freely to obey or disobey God. Lucifer, for reasons we may never be able to fathom, took such pride in his beauty, brilliance and exalted position that eventually he decided he deserved to occupy God's throne as sole ruler of the universe (Isaiah 14:12–15; Ezekiel 28:12–19). It was the first and only attempted *coup d'etat* in heaven. It failed. Lucifer was thrown out of heaven and one-third of God's angels (who had joined in his rebellion) were banished with him.

Where did they go? Look around! Satan is now "prince of this world." Our planet is under his control. It operates according to his rules. It is, in a very real sense, Satan's own personal kingdom, and his plan is that every human being will worship and obey him instead of God. His script hasn't changed, you see; only the cast and location have.

Who gave the devil so much power in our world? Not God! God created the world and turned it over to *us*, the people He made in His own image, the people He endowed with free wills so we could freely choose to love and obey Him. He entrusted the world to our care, and we gave it to Satan. Year after year, century after century, we have believed the devil's lies, allowed him to take more and more prisoners, more and more territory, and even attributed at times the work of his hands to God, since God is sovereign and His ways past searching out!

Now even those of us who refuse to give Satan an inch are forced to live in a world he dominates. The planet God lovingly created to be His own peaceable kingdom has been overrun by the enemy, and all of us are paying the devil's price. Christians, in particular.

That's because from the devil's point of view, we are the flies in the ointment. The way he sees it, we Christians are the only real threat to his power. Perhaps worse, we are a continual reminder of his failure. Every time the devil sees a Christian, he remembers that he will never occupy God's throne. This world is the only kingdom he will ever get the chance to control. Imagine his outrage when he finds that some of us are actually willing to lay down our lives to take this kingdom away from him and make it God's instead! How *dare* we?

We are, to be sure, a small and often disorganized army, but Satan still has good reason to be afraid of us. We have access to all the authority and power of God, and we have—as the devil well knows—a mighty angelic host on our side that vastly outnumbers his own. As you'll recall, Satan took only one-third of the angels with him when he fell, and he cannot create any more. Two-thirds of the angels, therefore, are still on God's side—and ours. You can be sure Satan never forgets that sobering fact. Neither should we.

Naturally, the devil finds this whole situation more than intolerable. It infuriates him. We Christians are the only thing standing between him and total domination of his planetary kingdom. If it were not for us, he would have the pleasure of saying to God at the Last Judgment, "You see? All the people You created have chosen me instead of You!"

But there's one thing even worse from Satan's standpoint—one thing that makes him tremble not only with rage, but with fear: the knowledge that we as the Body of Christ can join together with the unbreakable bond of love and take up arms against him, challenging his power with all the authority God has placed in our hands. We can do to him and his lackeys what the Rumanian people did in 1989 to the evil regime that had oppressed them for years: We can rise up as one and pull him off his throne. We can, by the authority of God, smash him and his evil army.

Satan's goal, then, is to prevent that at all costs from happening. He must keep the world and its inhabitants in darkness so they have no opportunity to know and experience God's love. If he can do that, Christians will never know God has given them the authority and means to take back the world and rescue those Satan holds captive—and his evil reign will continue.

In this way Satan still holds out hope that he can ruin God's plan for the new heaven and new earth reserved for those who freely choose to love and worship Him.

Satan is well aware that very few people will choose to follow him if they know who he is and understand their alternative. So he puts all his energy into keeping the light of the truth from shining in the darkness. And he is frantic to stop Christians from using our authority against him.

Satan's Strategies

What are some of the strategies Satan uses to accomplish this goal? There are six I would like to look at that have proved most successful. Only after we have examined these strategies will we look (in the next chapter) at some strategies of God's design for us to defeat him. Clearly we *can* win—if we know what we're up against and understand how to use the weapons God has provided. Greater is He that is in us than he that is in the world! (See 1 John 4:1–4.)

Number 1: The devil tries to block Christians' power against him by keeping us from our power source, keeping us from praying.

This is one of Satan's most important strategies. He will stop at nothing to disrupt our ability to communicate with God, to get to know Him and His will. It is through prayer that we join forces with our Commander-in-Chief and attack the enemy's strongholds. (One way we can gauge the effectiveness of our prayers, in fact, is to observe how hard the devil tries to stop them!)

How does he keep us from praying? By isolating us—

both from God and from one another. Isolation is a tried-and-true military strategy. If he can isolate us from God, he effectively cuts off our supply line (the power of the Holy Spirit), weakens our defenses and keeps us from getting our orders from headquarters.

Isolation from our fellow Christians is also critical for demonic forces because "where two or more are gathered together" to pray in the name of Jesus Christ, all the power of heaven is focused and released against them. Thus, while Satan works overtime to keep us from praying *individually*, he works a hundred times harder to keep us from praying *together* with other believers. Our united prayers spell disaster for him. They constitute the greatest threat to his power.

The way Satan goes about isolating us from God and one another almost always involves tempting us to sin. Why? Because when we do sin, there is a chance we won't confess it. And nothing separates us from God more than unconfessed sin. I have found that Satan usually tempts us to sin in two areas that have proven most fruitful for him throughout history:

—*Power.* Satan is especially clever at placing us in positions that give us a taste of power, because he knows we will probably hunger for more. Once we taste power, Satan puffs up our pride. We become more and more like him—and less and less aware of our dependency upon God. The rise of the occult in our time is a good example of what this temptation is all about. Satan has been able to draw millions into occult practices— horoscopes, palm-reading, tarot cards, ouiji boards, seances, witchcraft, the New Age movement—by convincing us that through these means we can gain control over our own lives and those of others.

Occult practices are Satan's phony substitutes for the genuine relationship we were created to have with God through prayer and an understanding of His Word. They also appeal to our curiosity about the future. There is an overwhelming desire in many people to know what tomorrow will bring. I wonder how many stop to think how boring and pointless, how predictable their existence would be if they actually knew? Millions of people will complain on the one hand about the predictability of their daily lives, while on the other hand they open their newspapers to the horoscope looking for answers that ostensibly will remove all the mystery and excitement that remain!

But the appeal of the occult has never been logical. Its drawing power is similar, I suppose, to the fake gemstones that are so popular today. "Even a jeweler can't tell the difference!" the advertisements say. "Looks exactly like a real diamond!"—or emerald, or ruby. If it looks exactly the same, why is the fake so cheap while the real thing is so expensive? And why are many people still willing to sacrifice to own the real thing?

The truth is, people who don't understand the value of the real thing will buy what *looks* expensive primarily so they can fool others into believing they own the genuine article! Deception is at the bottom of it all. This is the appeal of the occult, regardless of the masks it wears. It lures people into accepting glittery substitutes for spirituality that look real, but in the end only keep us separated from God.

—*Pleasure.* This second area in which Satan tempts us to sin is powerful because God created us with a tremendous capacity for pleasure. When we are in right relationship with Him, we can experience pleasure of a kind unknown to anyone but God's friends (and infinitely more is promised to us in the next world!). But Satan finds he can often get us to settle instead for pathetic and perverted substitutes.

We are, as C. S. Lewis said, like children who keep making mudpies in the slums because we can't imagine what is meant by the offer of a holiday by the seashore. Pleasure is especially effective as a means to draw us into sin because we will do almost anything to get it. We will degrade and humiliate and even kill ourselves and others to obtain a fleeting moment of it. Research scientists have found that when laboratory animals are allowed to self-administer cocaine whenever they want, they increase their ingestion quickly to the point at which they receive nonstop injections of the drug—until finally their hearts simply burst. They kill themselves literally out of an insatiable desire for more and more pleasure.

Human beings do the same thing. Thousands die every year from drug overdoses because they are addicted to pleasure and will stop at nothing to get it. Incredibly, many pregnant women refuse to deny themselves the pleasure of drugs even when they know their babies will die as a result. Satan knows how easy it is to tempt us in this area.

Promiscuous and perverted sex, of course, falls under the same category—everything from pornography to rape to child molestation and a thousand variations in between. Sex can be overwhelmingly magnetic and addictive to people who don't understand how it can seduce us away from God.

Money and possessions also fall into this category. When John D. Rockefeller, one of the world's wealthiest men, was asked by a reporter, "How much money is enough?" he replied with a sad smile, "Just a little more."

Remember: Pleasure in itself is not evil, any more than power or sex or money or possessions are. It's when we love these things instead of God—or when we want them so much we are willing to disobey God to have them—that they become idols for us. Satan loves to tempt us with perverted substitutes for the pleasures God has promised to give us through our relationship with Him.

When Satan can't tempt us to sin with power or pleasure, he will use other, more subtle ploys, such as introducing doubt into our minds to disable our faith. If we lose our faith we are obviously more likely to sin. He is still whispering to us the same question he asked Eve: "Has God *really* said. . . ?"

If he does manage to isolate us through sin, he will try to make that isolation permanent by convincing us that we can never be forgiven. So, while we should always be alert to temptations to sin, we must never let Satan fool us into believing that sin has placed us in a hopeless position, because that will *truly* defeat us. God is always ready to restore us when we seek His forgiveness.

If he cannot get us to stop using our authority against him by keeping us from praying, the devil often takes a more cunning approach.

Number 2: He tries to convince us that we can believe God but not obey Him.

This is something I have experienced myself. As an example, Satan will suggest—either directly or through other people (perhaps even Christians)—that God doesn't really expect me to go to dangerous places like Beirut, even though I know God has called me to go there, and even though He has confirmed that my usefulness to Him lies in ministering in such places.

Sometimes I find thoughts running through my mind that go something like this: "Andrew, you're too valuable to the cause of Christ to place yourself in such a risky position. After all, you're no good to the Body of Christ if you die! It would be much wiser to stay home and use the knowledge you have gained to teach others who are younger and stronger. This way you can multiply your ministry. Haven't you done enough? God knows you believe Him, and even if He *has* told you to go to Lebanon and all these other terrible places, He'll understand if you decide to stay home now and put your talents to work in other, less dangerous ways."

Do you see how subtle this kind of tactic can be? I have no doubt that millions of potential missionaries and evangelists have been neutralized by this same approach.

"Sure," Satan whispers, "God might have said, 'Go into all the world and preach the Gospel,' but did He say *everyone* should go? That would be unreasonable! If everyone went, who would be left in church?" (A terrific question, by the way! If our churches were doing what they should, they would be empty except for new converts and trainees, because the others would be leaving to do what God commanded them to do! That would be the first day the neighborhood would take the church seriously. As a result I am sure the church would be filled again the next week with new converts.)

But Satan likes to take this strategy a step further: "You can believe God and obey Him just by 'letting your light shine'—by looking after your family and taking care of your job responsibilities and living a life that sets a good example. You don't have to tell people about Jesus. You don't have to intercede for others. You don't have to give to the Lord's work or involve yourself in fighting against drugs, abortion, the occult, political corruption or pornography. There's no need for you to sacrifice yourself that way." This leads to Satan's third ploy to stop Christians from using our authority against him.

Number 3: He tries to convince us that we have a right to be happy.

No, we are not entitled to be "happy"—at least not in human terms. We are not entitled to a happy family, a nice house, beauty, prosperity, popularity or fame. God has, in fact, told us that in this world we will find our only real happiness in knowing Him and becoming involved in His plans.

I'll never forget the time I was ministering in a private home in the capital city of an Eastern European country in the sixties. I was teaching from the Scriptures to a sizeable group of Christians who were desperately hungry for the Word of God. While I was talking, the door opened and to my surprise an old friend of mine walked in. His name was Karl. I had thought he was still in prison. I'd worked with Karl in another country where the churches were—and still are—being bulldozed, believers are being imprisoned and Bibles are being destroyed. Karl had been arrested for evangelizing and sentenced to prison for three years. Now here I was in another city, and Karl walked in the door!

I was overjoyed, as you can imagine. We jumped around and hugged and cried, as you always do on such an occasion.

Eventually we all settled down, but we became very quiet because I found I just couldn't talk anymore. I wanted to listen instead of talk; I knew Karl could teach all of us more than I could. Everyone there knew that one day they, too, would have to pay the price Karl had paid, so they hung on his every word. He talked about his experiences in prison for a while and then turned to me, the only foreigner in the group. "Andrew," he said, "are there any pastors in Holland in prison for their faith?"

No one had ever asked me such a strange question, but I didn't have to think about my answer because I knew that if any pastor was in prison in Holland, it was because he wasn't a good Christian pastor—not because he was. "No," I told him.

I could see that my answer was painful to Karl. In his country, only the good Christians were in prison. He thought about this for a minute and then asked me, "Why not?"

I was really getting nervous by this time. How could I explain this to my brothers and sisters who were living under persecution? I started talking about all the freedoms we have—all the Christian book shops we have, all the Bibles we can own, how we can preach in our churches every hour of the week if we want to, how we can shout it from the rooftops, go into the streets, preach on television and radio and in magazines. I told them that in Holland I use all those means to preach the Good News, and I said I can even go out and invite my neighbors to come to church with me. In Karl's country, you could go to prison for three years for doing that. I said, "We can talk to the people we work with about Jesus. We can give Bibles to anyone."

Then I looked around and saw that those people could not understand what I was saying. It was beyond their comprehension. Suddenly I felt ashamed. I was making a fool of myself talking to these persecuted believers about such things. So I stopped talking. But I felt Karl's strangely blue eyes and serious face focused on me. After several minutes of silence he opened his mouth and said, "If all this is true, then tell me, Andrew: What do you in Holland do with 2 Timothy 3:12?"

It was obviously one of his favorite verses, but I didn't know it from memory, so I had to look it up. I opened my Bible and read it out loud. I will never forget what

God said there: "Everyone who wants to live a godly life in Christ Jesus will be persecuted. . . ." In the preceding verse, I noticed, persecution was mentioned two more times.

I was speechless for several minutes. Then I reacted in a way probably typical of the way most of us in the free world would have reacted in that situation. I turned into an instant theologian and began to explain that this verse applied to the early Church because Paul spoke specifically about the places where he had been beaten and put in prison, so it really referred to that period two thousand years ago, not to today. I was getting more nervous by the minute.

After I looked around at the sad, incredulous faces that surrounded me, I sighed and said, "These verses probably do apply today to restricted countries like yours. And to countries where revolution and war cause this same kind of suffering. But in Holland and America, and in other free countries, we do not suffer persecution for our faith. Why should we?"

I was sweating by this time. I stopped talking, and nobody said anything for a long time. Karl just kept looking at me with those piercing blue eyes of his. I read the verse again and again. *Everyone*, it said. *Everyone who wants to live a godly life in Christ Jesus will be persecuted.*

It hit me right between the eyes. We who live in the "free" world are not exempt. If we are not being persecuted, we should be asking ourselves Karl's question: *Why not?* More than half the population of the world today cannot take the Word of God seriously and live a godly life in Christ Jesus without being persecuted or imprisoned or killed for it.

Finally I looked up at Karl, whose eyes were still riveted on me. "Forgive me, Karl," I said, "but we do nothing with that verse."

He shook his head sadly, and so did I.

That moment will remain with me forever. It was a powerful reminder of a fact Satan wants us to forget: We are living in enemy territory, all of us—not just those in the restricted nations of the world. And if we love God and are living as Jesus taught us, we will be persecuted, reviled, hated, laughed at, or perhaps even imprisoned or killed for our faith. We will not be the toast of the town, we will not be heroes—except perhaps in a limited way among those in the minority who are also living for God. We will certainly not be applauded or even tolerated by the enemies of God.

So we must keep a proper perspective, remembering that we have all eternity to be happy. Happiness should not even be a consideration for us here. Jesus warned every believer that "in this world you will have trouble" (John 16:33). This doesn't mean that our lives will necessarily be one long stretch of unrelenting agony—although for many Christians today, this is the case. But we cannot forget that our enemy will not leave us alone to live lives of quiet harmony with our God. He will attack us constantly if we threaten him in any way by trying to change God's mind about allowing his activity.

Number 4: Satan tries to stop Christians by engendering fear—either fear on an individual level (like fear of witnessing to your neighbor or co-worker) or fear on a national level.

Satan is a master intimidator. He creates the oppressive, cruel political systems like Communism and fascism that seek to destroy all knowledge of God and make people afraid even to pray. Hundreds of millions of people have been cut off from the preaching of the Gospel for most of the twentieth century through this means. We can't forget that even with the advent of *glasnost* and *perestroika* in the Soviet Union, millions around the world still cannot read the Bible or speak the name of Christ without fear of torture, imprisonment or death.

Satan also inspires false religious systems that control whole nations and bring terrible suffering to Christians living in those lands. Such systems often send the Church underground. Even in many Western nations today, the influence of false religious systems has started to make it difficult for Christians to preach the Gospel. When they insist that salvation is found in Christ alone, they are attacked as "narrowminded, intolerant bigots."

I see this happening more and more. Recently a man on a television talk show in America got a big round of applause from the audience when he chatted about his recent conversion to a mystical Eastern religion and said, "I'm convinced that there is only one real sin, and that's narrowmindedness." His implication was, of course, that Christians—who contend there is only one God and only one way to know Him—are the worst sinners of all. I wonder who put that idea into his head?

I have often told my Christian friends in the restricted nations that they had better prepare themselves for missionary work, because soon we will be looking to them to help us. Those of us in the Western world who have never really suffered for our faith are going to face the reality of 2 Timothy 3:12. We are going to find ourselves the objects of persecution and ridicule and scorn of a sort that we have not experienced before, because we are in a weakened, vulnerable condition. If we don't prepare ourselves for what we are going to face in the next decade, I shudder to think what could happen. The more I see of what Satan is doing today, the more convinced I am of this.

Number 5: Satan tries to neutralize Christians by sowing seeds of dissension, accusation, anger, mistrust or bitterness among the brethren. This breaks the bond of loving unity and keeps Christians distracted and unable to organize for a counterattack. In other words, if the enemy can get us fighting among ourselves, we won't be able to fight him.

Churches and Christian organizations are not, as a rule, destroyed by opposition from outside. In fact, attack from the outside usually cements relationships and draws believers together, mobilizing them for battle. Satan has learned that the best way to attack groups of believers is to work from the inside. He disguises himself as an angel of light or sends his messengers as "servants of righteousness" to create confusion and mistrust, often working on just one or two individuals to begin with. Then, slowly, he stirs up bitterness, anger, envy—all the nasty attitudes that isolate us and keep our eyes off the Lord.

I have heard countless stories of prayer groups and Bible studies that have been destroyed by these means—usually just when the group is on the brink of a tremendous breakthrough. How does this happen?

In one fairly typical case I heard about, a new couple came into a Bible study and prayer group that had been meeting together for several years. Ron and Carla (we'll call them) seemed somehow more "spiritually qualified" for leadership than any who were already involved—partly because of their vast knowledge of Scripture, partly because they seemed to have special insights and gifts to provide the kind of leadership and direction the group thought they needed, and partly because of the sheer force of their personalities.

So they quickly became the unofficial leaders. Ron and Carla flashed lots of "spiritual credit cards"—stories of miraculously answered prayers, prophetic dreams, visions and direct "words from the Lord" that suggested to the group that soon they were going to have a powerful impact on their community for the Lord.

Very soon, however, members of the group began to get calls and visits from Carla and Ron. The purpose of these visits was always the same: to hint—very gently at first—that certain other members were hindering the progress of the group. These members, Ron and Carla suggested, were not on the same high spiritual plane as the rest of the group because they did not accept the agenda God had clearly given the group through the couple. The group would be better off, therefore, without these members.

After a long and agonizing struggle, several members began to discern what was happening. They met together, prayed and confronted Carla and Ron with what they had been doing. Naturally, the couple counter-attacked, accusing those who confronted them of being un-Christian and out of tune with the Holy Spirit. Over a period of several weeks the group struggled to continue, but eventually—sadly—they decided simply to disband. Too much distrust had been sown and too many members hurt too badly to continue. Ron and Carla went off (presumably to join another prayer group) claiming that they had been the victims of demonic attack.

Tragically, they didn't know how right they were. Satan's "messengers" are also his victims. He hates them as much as he hates us—and they suffer in their own ways even more than we do.

Number 6: When these strategies fail, Satan may resort to direct attack to keep us from using our authority against him.

This can take many forms, but physical or emotional attacks on us or our families are among the most common. I have witnessed and experienced these kinds of battles so often that they have become almost routine.

I remember a story told to me by a preacher's widow about her husband, who was a pastor-evangelist in Eastern Europe many years ago while she remained back home. Everywhere he preached they experienced tremendous revival. Then one night, just before he got up to preach, a telegram was handed to the pastor: "Come home. Your wife is dying." The preacher, an experienced spiritual warrior, recognized what was happening. After praying about it for a few moments he announced, "That's not God. He will not let my wife die when He's called me here to preach. I'm not going home. She will not die." He asked for prayer on his wife's behalf, and went on to complete his scheduled meetings. By the time he returned home, his wife had recovered.

After recounting this story to me, the widow smiled at me and said, "You see, he knew God, and he knew what God would and would not do. When you know Him that way, you have the liberty to say yes or no without fear. My husband was certain that only Satan would attempt to keep him from preaching the Gospel to people who might have no other chance to hear. So he had to stay. He couldn't give the devil that kind of victory. And he was able to trust God completely in spite of the devil's attack."

In a sense, attacks like these should encourage us. They are a sign that the enemy has run out of more subtle options and has become desperate to stop us. But physical and emotional attacks can be frustrating, debilitating, painful and—if we don't identify them for what they are—they can cause us to lose heart. So we must be on guard against them.

Most of the time, I have found, the sickness and injuries Satan throws at us can be categorized as harassment more than anything else. Remember, he wants us to suffer because he thinks that will cause us to turn our backs on God or give up our efforts for Him. When he sees that he can't achieve his objectives that way, however, he usually gives up. Thus, it's important that we persevere through this kind of suffering and refuse to submit to his threats and harassment.

It's also wise to understand, when we are under this kind of attack and in emotional or physical pain, that we usually cannot pray effectively for ourselves. Effective prayer, as I have said, requires focus, and focus is the first thing to go when we are in pain. Most of the time we can think of nothing but our own suffering, and that's perfectly normal. When this happens, we must count on other Christians to pray for us. The first thing I do in such a situation is to call my favorite prayer partners and ask them to take up my cause. It gives me great comfort to imagine how this must frustrate the enemy!

There's much more we could say about the devil's strategies, but I think we have covered enough to give us a clear picture of the spiritual warfare in which we are engaged. Let's move on now and look at the final exciting question of how we can defeat our enemy!

7
How We Can Defeat the Enemy

A couple of years ago at an Open Doors prayer conference, an old friend was talking to me over dinner about how hard it is to present the Gospel in a world controlled by evil powers. "I know we must become more confrontational and aggressive," he said. "But how can we manage to battle the enemy in a hostile world and still represent nothing but the love of Christ?"

I answered him by telling a story about the time Corrie ten Boom and I were in a meeting in Holland in which the group was discussing the same problem. Somehow we had gotten off on a tangent into a conversation about thermostats for heating and cooling systems. It was not such a strange tangent, really, when you consider that Corrie was fascinated by everything technical. She was, as you remember, a watchmaker by trade, and she loved anything that moved—from watches to people and everything in between.

As it happened, everyone in the room that day seemed to know something about thermostats, and Corrie was bent on understanding how they worked. Once we satisfied her curiosity, Corrie said, "Tell me, what's the difference between a thermostat and a thermometer?"

Several more minutes of explanation followed, until Corrie's eyes lit up with understanding and she began to nod. "Yes, I see," she said. "A thermometer only indicates what the temperature is. But a thermostat changes the temperature." Then she practically jumped out of her chair. "Andrew!" she exclaimed. "That's the answer to our problem! We've got to be thermostats—not thermometers!"

As usual, Corrie hit the bull's-eye. In a world like ours it's always much easier—even for a Christian—to be a thermometer instead of a thermostat. All of us read the newspapers or watch television and observe the international and local events—war, revolution, hostage-taking, crime, government corruption, ethical bankruptcy. We see the decline in moral and spiritual values reflected everywhere. We can even observe the positive things—the open doors in Russia and Eastern Europe and other parts of the world that have been closed to the Gospel for decades, the release of those who have been imprisoned in Communist gulags and mental hospitals for their faith.

But if we only observe these conditions from day to day, if we only make note of them and say, "It's terrible" or "It's wonderful," we're nothing more than thermometers. And Corrie was right: If we're going to win the war against Satan, if we're going to beseech God to change His mind about what He allows the devil to do in this world, we must be more than thermometers. We must be thermostats.

Thermostats exist to change the situation. They don't merely register that it's too cold or too hot; they respond to our touch and actually alter the environment. In my office in the wintertime I can hear a little *click* in the thermostat when it goes on, and if I'm watching for it I can even see a little spark fly to make the connection. Then the central boiler swings into action and—boom!— something changes. The whole mechanism of my heating system will fight the cold because I made a decision: I decided how warm it should be in my office, and the thermostat responded by changing the temperature.

This is exactly what we must do as Christians. We must understand that we were not created to be mere thermometers for the world, shaking our heads or clucking our tongues over how hot or cold it's getting. We were created to respond to the Holy Spirit's touch by clicking on, firing up our boilers and causing change! God has placed in our hands the power and authority to do that.

Jesus spent a lot of time teaching His disciples how to defeat Satan. He also set the example for all of us who follow Him, because He managed to defeat Satan on his own battleground, and at the same time to love the world's inhabitants as no one ever had. Jesus was—to use Corrie's analogy—the perfect thermostat. Wherever He went, He responded to His Father's touch by causing drastic changes.

The story of Jesus' temptation in the wilderness (Matthew 4:1–11; Mark 1:13; Luke 4:1–13) teaches one of the most important of all principles regarding spiritual warfare. Let's look briefly at the Gospel of Luke to see the strategy Jesus used to defeat the devil.

When the devil first approached Jesus after His forty-day fast he said, "If you are the Son of God, tell this stone to become bread." Satan knew perfectly well, of course, that there were no ifs about it. He was there because of who Jesus was! Jesus had nothing to prove to the devil, so His counterattack was both simple and direct: "It is written: 'Man does not live on bread alone.' "

When Satan next approached Him, offering the largest bribe in history, Jesus didn't change His strategy. He struck back using His most potent weapon: "It is written: 'Worship the Lord your God and serve him only.' "

By now Satan saw that he wasn't getting anywhere with his standard approaches. He decided to fight fire with fire. In his third attack he quoted Scripture to Jesus, twisting it to serve his own nasty purpose (one of his favorite tactics throughout the ages, by the way, and one he still employs with great success). This time he took Jesus to the top of the Temple in Jerusalem. "If you are the Son of God," he said, "throw yourself down from here. For it is written: 'He will command his angels concerning you to guard you carefully; they will lift you up in their hands, so that you will not strike your foot against a stone.' "

Can you imagine? Satan had the gall to attack the Word of God by quoting the Word *to* the Word! Notice, however, that the devil did *not* quote the Scripture correctly. He omitted "to guard you in all your ways" (see Psalm 91:11), thus falsifying God's Word. Had Jesus succumbed to this temptation He would have walked away from the center of God's will—and from God's protection, as well.

A stunning example of Satan's arrogance. But Jesus was ready for him again. He replied, in essence, "The Scripture also says, 'Do not tempt the Lord your God.' " It was a duel between Jesus and Satan, and their swords, in this case, were the Scriptures! But Satan realized quickly that he was out of his depth, and he departed to lick his wounds.

Do you see how Jesus fought Satan in this hour of temptation by using the Scriptures as His weapon? The Bible doesn't list all of the specific temptations Jesus was subjected to during His face-off with the devil, but it does say in another place that He was tempted "in every way, just as we are—yet . . . without sin" (Hebrews 4:15). And from the three examples given, it is clear that Jesus' primary weapon was Scripture.

In each of these examples in the Gospel record, we should also note that Satan hoped to tempt Jesus to sin by using His power selfishly—to feed Himself after a forty-day fast, to prove Himself God's Son and to gain power in the world. But Satan vastly underestimated God's wisdom and selfless love, and even more vastly overestimated his own cleverness. (This has always been the devil's downfall.)

Satan is still using this same ploy today. As we saw in the last chapter, he likes to tempt us with power because he understands its appeal better than anyone. The moment we become Christians and gain access to God's power through our relationship with Him, Satan will jump in immediately and try to corrupt us by tempting us to use that power selfishly. If he can get us to spend our time praying for selfish things instead of interceding to "change the world's temperature" and defeat his strategies, he will have neutralized us.

It is written: That was the weapon Jesus chose to use in His confrontation with evil, and it was powerful enough to repel every temptation Satan brought His way. Jesus knew that the Word of God was His single best defense against all of Satan's temptations. It is ours as well.

I have always been a big advocate of Scripture memorization for this and many other reasons. I realize that memorization is out of fashion in many churches these days, especially in the free world where Bibles are available to everyone. "Why should we put the time and energy into memorizing," people say, "when we can open our Bibles and find whatever verses we want anytime we like?" Such people don't know how fortunate they are, and I'm afraid they don't understand how quickly such privileges can be taken away.

Nor do they realize *why* memorized Scriptures can give anyone a tremendous advantage in spiritual warfare. If enemy soldiers had kicked in your front door a few moments ago and lined up your family to be shot, would it help to shout at them, "I have a gun out in the garage"? No, if a weapon is going to be effective, it must be available where and when you need it.

Our best weapon against Satan is Scripture, and if it's going to be useful we can't keep it in the garage. When you memorize a Scripture you place it in the arsenal of weapons you carry with you. It's always right there in an emergency. In a surprise attack, you have at your command the potent, living Word that carries all the authority and power of God to repel the devil's soldiers and give you strength for combat.

I have known many people who have survived oppressive situations for years simply by recalling a few memorized verses from childhood. Others have had nothing more than bits and pieces passed on from believers who had memorized Scripture. In some places I've visited, underground Christians have pages torn from a Bible somebody was able to obtain, and everyone commits his page to memory before exchanging it with someone else. Sometimes the pages are never passed on or exchanged because believers can't bring themselves to give up the only Scripture they've ever had in their hands. It becomes their most precious treasure. When I walk into a group of believers like that, I find that as I open my own Bible, every eye in the room will be glued to the Book, as if it were a banquet table laid out before starving people.

In one Eastern European city a pastor told me of a young member of his underground church who, after receiving his single page of Scripture, stopped him on the street and said, "Pastor, now that I have my Scripture, I have hope!" The pastor asked which book of the Bible was represented on the young man's page, and he answered, "Jeremiah." The pastor replied, "But Jeremiah is not a very hopeful book—it's pretty depressing! How can a page from Jeremiah give you such hope?" The young man replied with great excitement, "Pastor, it says on that page that the word of the Lord came to Jeremiah. If the word of the Lord could come to Jeremiah, it can come to me, too!"

It is often among believers like this that I find the most profound, earth-shaking faith I've ever encountered. They may know only one page—or one verse—of Scripture, but it's enough to carry them to triumph in the midst of the worst sufferings Satan can invent! Those of us who have all the Bibles we want seldom seem to appreciate the dynamite we hold in our hands.

Many years ago—in 1966, I believe it was—I attended the first World Congress on Evangelism, a gathering of several thousand dedicated missionaries and evangelists who met in Berlin to share modern strategies for reaching mankind with the Gospel. My most vivid memory of that Congress was the moment when Rachel Saint, the South American missionary, stood at the podium with three primitive Auca Indians dressed in the colorful garb of their people. They were some of the first Christians in their tribe, which had been struggling to survive in its isolated jungle habitat and for most of the century had been considered one of the most unreachable tribes in Ecuador.

Someone asked these Indian Christians if they would tell the audience their favorite verses of Scripture. Everyone expected them to recite John 3:16 or some other basic verse relating to salvation, since most of the Bible had not yet been translated into their language. But the Indians had a surprise for us. They looked at each other, conferred briefly, and then one of them stepped forward, declaring with a broad smile, "Devil get out, and never come back!" It brought down the house.

I remember thinking as I watched this how until that moment most of the more "sophisticated" Christians gathered for that Congress had failed to take into account one crucial aspect of the Gospel we had been called to preach. It was this aspect that turned out to be the most powerful and life-changing one as far as these struggling Indian people were concerned: Jesus came into the world not only to express God's love and reconcile us to the Father. He also came to say, "Devil get out, and never come back!" It took three "primitive" Christians to cut through to the heart of the matter for the rest of us. Since then, I have often used their free translation of that verse (Mark 9:25) in my own battles with the devil!

I'm always encouraged when I remember that the apostle Paul said, "We wanted to come to you . . . but Satan stopped us" (1 Thessalonians 2:18). There are casualties on both sides in any war, and even though we know we're on the winning side in this war, we must be honest and mature enough to recognize that we will occasionally lose a battle. We have become so success- and victory-oriented that we think we shame our Lord if we admit a defeat.

Nothing is further from the truth. After all, the life of the Church on earth will end as did Jesus' life on earth: on a cross. There will not be a victorious Christian sweep of all the dirt from the floor of our world. But the seeming defeat of Jesus on the cross was His greatest victory, and it is ours as well. We must come to grips with God's point of view.

God is able to transform our defeats into victories as we learn from our mistakes with the wisdom and in- sight He provides. As someone has said, "That which does not destroy me makes me stronger." God takes the long view, and so must we. Although Satan inevitably wins a few battles in each of our lives, if we are mature we can go back to the place where we lost touch with God's will, or where Satan caught us unprepared, and ask God to help us make a new start. There's nothing wrong with that. God doesn't expect us to be perfect; "he knows how we are formed, he remembers that we are dust" (Psalm 103:14). Our setbacks and losses can ultimately teach us—and those who follow us—how to win bigger and even more important battles in the fu- ture.

There are five simple principles I believe we should keep in mind as we involve ourselves in combat with the enemy through prayer. In my own experience, these five principles can bring victory in all spiritual warfare. Remember: We will win the fight, even though we may sometimes lose a round to the devil. Setbacks and losses should not discourage or deter us, because the ultimate victory belongs to Christ and, through Him, to us.

Number 1: We must arm ourselves for battle.

This is a very basic and practical principle. Most of us have read (or even memorized!) Paul's instructions to the church at Ephesus regarding spiritual warfare:

> Be strong in the Lord and in his mighty power. Put on the full armor of God so that you can take your stand against the devil's schemes. For our struggle is not against flesh and blood, but against the . . . powers of this dark world and against the spiritual forces of evil in the heavenly realms. Therefore put on the full armor of God, so that when the day of evil comes, you may be able to stand your ground, and after you have done everything, to stand. Stand firm then, with the belt of truth buckled around your waist, with the breastplate of righteousness in place, and with your feet fitted with the readiness that comes from the gospel of peace. In addition to all this, take up the shield of faith, with which you can extinguish all the flaming arrows of the evil one. Take the helmet of salvation and the sword of the Spirit, which is the word of God. And pray in the Spirit on all occasions with all kinds of prayers and requests. With this in mind, be alert and always keep on praying for all the saints.
>
> Ephesians 6:10–18

Nothing could be more straightforward than this. If I must go to an important meeting and I know there's a storm in progress outside, I first dress to protect myself from the elements, and then I go. It's only common sense. Paul is telling us here to do exactly that: There's a storm outside, so dress for it before you walk into it. If you don't, you'll get soaked!

The application of Paul's instructions in this passage involves a spiritual leap from the theoretical to the practical. The armor must be worn consistently and deliberately if it's going to be effective:

—We must live the truth. That means we must speak the truth, defend the truth and, if necessary, be willing to die for the truth—as so many heroes of faith before us have done. Lies can have no place in our lives, because Satan is the father of lies—the deceiver.

—We must live righteously. Our God is righteous, and as He dwells in us we will reflect His character more and more. We are, of course, made righteous through Christ's sacrifice on the cross, but as members of His Body we must also strive to live according to His commands. This means that we must choose to live righteous lives whatever the cost, allowing God to reign in all that we do. Even if the whole world seems to embrace evil, we must be committed to standing as beacons of righteousness, supporting all who do right and speaking up for what is good. As the saying goes, "I'm the only Jesus some people will ever see." We must, therefore, allow Him to live His life in and through us in an uncompromising way.

—We must equip ourselves as well to proclaim the Gospel of peace. We must be messengers always ready to tell others about Christ. It is through the sharing of the Gospel that Satan's hold on mankind is broken and God's Kingdom is strengthened and enlarged.

—We must shield ourselves with faith. Faith, as the writer of Hebrews says, is "being sure of what we hope for and certain of what we do not see" (Hebrews 11:1). Through faith we see what others cannot, both in God's Kingdom and in Satan's. This enables us, among many other things, to protect ourselves and others from the invisible rulers, authorities and powers that control this dark world.

—We must wear the helmet salvation provides. The knowledge that we are saved and will spend eternity with Jesus can protect our minds from despair and help build our resilience.

—We must carry the sword of the Lord—His Word. Again, the Word was Jesus' most potent weapon, and it must be ours as well.

—We must pray continually (see also 1 Thessalonians 5:17). Is this really possible or practical? Probably not in a literal sense, but I believe the apostle is saying that our attitude can be one of constant attentiveness to God's Spirit. "Always keep on praying for all the saints," he says, much the way our mothers used to tell us, "Always take your umbrella." We must not only carry an umbrella to cover ourselves, but to cover our brothers and sisters as well. We are in this storm together.

We can pray and listen to God, just as we can worship

Him anywhere at all—while we're putting diapers on the baby or fighting traffic on the freeway, while we're typing letters in our offices or walking on the beach. There is nowhere we cannot pray if we commit ourselves to it.

A good friend of mine, Geoffrey Bull, who along with George Patterson was the last remaining missionary in Tibet when the Communists took over, was imprisoned for three years in a horrible prison. He was so tortured and shattered mentally by his captors that finally he could not think anymore. He told me that when his mind at last grew so paralyzed that he could not even pray coherent prayers, he said to God, "Lord, if I can somehow stand up in the center of my cell, will You accept that as an act of worship?" Each day thereafter until he was released, Geoff managed to pull himself to his feet in the center of his cell, silent and yielded before God. That was his prayer and his worship.

If Geoffrey Bull could find a way to pray even when he couldn't *think*, I believe it's safe to say that prayer is possible in any situation.

I am convinced, in fact, that we can pray even when we sleep. Many times I've awakened with a keen awareness of having just interceded for someone. I think it is not only possible but likely that the Holy Spirit can move us to pray in our spirits while our minds are asleep. Who knows? These may even be our best prayers!

Number 2: We must resist the devil and he will flee from us (James 4:7).

This second principle is so obvious it is easy to forget.

Exactly what does it mean? Various references offer words like these as synonyms for *resist:* combat, challenge, dispute, duel, oppose, repel, assail, assault, attack, contradict, impugn, baffle, frustrate, thwart, hinder, obstruct.

Get the picture? Resisting the devil means much more than just saying no to temptation, although that's part of it. It means more than asking God to rebuke him, although that, too, is often involved. Know and understand that since Calvary we have *more* authority than the archangel Michael. (See Jude 9.) Resisting also encompasses far more than saying, "Devil get out, and never come back!"

It means we act like thermostats: We cause changes in the situation by refusing to take the devil's attacks lying down. We go on the offensive against the devil in every possible way—through our prayers and through our Spirit-inspired actions. Using the Word of God as our sword and wearing the whole armor of God, we contend forcefully for the faith. We say, "I am against this!" when we encounter evil, and we take action to oppose wickedness in every form. We say, "I am for this!" as we uphold righteousness and justice. In other words, *we refuse to give the devil an inch of ground in our world without a fight*—always remembering that people are not our enemies.

An interviewer on Christian television once asked me, "Andrew, do you think the Communists are our biggest enemies or the Arabs? Or the terrorists and revolutionaries and drug traffickers?" I replied, "They are not our enemies." The interviewer looked shocked. She said, "But then who *is* our enemy?" I said, "The devil." She seemed more shocked! Even those of us who are on the front lines can forget this important truth. This leads us to our next principle.

Number 3: We must learn how to pray for and how to pray against.

By this I mean we can break down the powers of evil and build up the righteous through our prayers. Let me give you a couple of examples from my own experience.

I have been teaching many pastors in Eastern Europe in recent years. One of the things I do is take them up on hills or mountains that overlook their cities and we pray *for* the city, for all the inhabitants, for those who love God and live righteously. We bless them. We name those we know who are aiding the suffering Church, and we bless those we don't know who are quietly serving God's purposes. Then we pray *against* the evil powers that hold the city in bondage.

I took an old friend named Stefanoff with me above the city of Plovdiv, Bulgaria, a city that had no church. We looked out on the city from that vantage point and prayed against the oppression that was keeping the city in bondage, against the powers of darkness, atheism, persecution and tyranny. We "bound the strong man," as Jesus said we should in Matthew 12:29, commanding evil spirits and demons to depart. Then we prayed for the souls of all the people and for the establishment of a church.

Our seven years of prayer for the U.S.S.R. was another example of praying for and praying against. Open Doors alone had at least three prayer chains going around the clock, day and night. Over a thousand people in each prayer chain were each praying at least ten minutes a day specifically *for* the release of new leadership in the U.S.S.R., *for* the opening of doors for prisoners, *for* opportunities to take Bibles to the people, *for* believers to be strengthened in specific ways and much more. We also prayed *against* the atheistic, oppressive powers and asked God to remove from power those who were enemies of the Church. And God answered!

I believe this kind of "for/against" prayer can be a highly effective strategy in spiritual warfare. I don't reserve it for special situations; I use it every day. When I'm driving or walking down the street and I see someone stopped at a traffic light or waiting at the curb next to me, I bless him or her. We should bless everyone who keeps the law. Even if I don't have any personal contact with others, I can still bless them. When I'm in an airplane I like to take the window seat because I can look out upon cities and farms and freeways and bless those people who are keeping the law. I do it in almost every imaginable circumstance. And when I bless anyone, he is blessed! I believe that. It's scriptural.

At the same time, there are certain circumstances—and this is a very tricky area—when praying against may involve a kind of prayer most of us have never even considered. I'm referring to the rare situations in which we can actually pray for the deaths of people who have sold their souls to Satan.

This is extreme—even frightening. And in light of what I said about people not being our enemies, it may even look as though I'm being inconsistent, not to say unloving. But I don't believe this is true. We should hope that people who are committed to the devil's active service will have every opportunity for repentance. But if they are too hardened to change, I believe we can ask God to change His mind about letting them continue to live.

There are exceptions to most rules—including God's. God's rule is love, but here is the exception: He does not love Satan or his demonic servants, nor does He love the evil that Satan perpetrates through those who are his slaves—and neither should we (Psalm 97:10; Amos 5:15; Romans 12:9). We certainly must not pray for anyone's demise without being sure of God's will in the matter, but there are occasions when I believe this kind of prayer is warranted.

We must recognize there are people in our world who are controlled completely by Satan. As long as they live, such people will do nothing but evil. As examples, I would cite both Hitler and Stalin. I've studied their lives in great detail. (My hobby is reading biographies, and I have hundreds of them in my library.) I can say without the slightest hesitation that both men sold themselves one hundred percent to the devil. I will go even further and say that anyone who prayed for either of them was wasting his breath.

I know this sounds shocking, because we are talking about drastic situations, about life-and-death prayers and about souls that cannot be redeemed. I am convinced there is nothing in the Scriptures that gives the slightest hint that men like Stalin or Hitler are redeemable. The Scriptures make it clear, in fact, that men like these should die, because they pollute and defile the earth with their violence and bloodshed, causing nothing but anguish and suffering to humanity (Numbers 35:31–33).

So, while I caution you again that we have to be *very* careful in this matter because we don't want to try to manipulate God for selfish purposes, I believe there are times when we can properly ask God to do more than remove certain people from positions of power. We can pray for the deaths of those who are remorseless and irredeemable murderers and persecutors of the innocent. I would include in this group the murderers of our children—leaders of drug cartels and child pornography rings, for example—as well as murderers who blatantly acknowledge that they worship Satan and do his bidding. Such people live only to destroy, and it is not God's will that they should do so.

You may remember the old story about the church members who prayed for God to show them how to get rid of the spiderwebs that covered the highest windows of the sanctuary. The church was forced regularly to hire a cleaning crew with special equipment to clear away the webs—an expense the church could not afford. After several weeks of intermittent prayer for guidance, one of the elders finally went to the heart of the problem by praying, "Lord, kill the spiders!" There are moments when we have a right and a responsibility to do the same.

We can also pray against systems. These are the organized evil empires we must learn to break down through prayer, because in tolerating them, we allow them to corrupt us. We must fight against them in every way we can. I would include in this category such diverse satanic systems as Communism, Islam and all the other evil, perverse cults and occultic religions that wreak havoc and destruction and terrorism wherever they gain a foothold.

How do we pray against such systems? We can express our opposition in a variety of ways. We can, as I suggested in the section on resisting the devil, say, "I am against this!" every time we find an opportunity—not only in prayer, but in public. This will help stir us up to holy indignation. We can have the courage to stand up and say, "This is not right! I won't accept it!" And then we can go out and do something about it.

We can also bind those systems by the authority of Jesus Christ. Remember Matthew 18:18: "Whatever you bind on earth will be bound in heaven, and whatever you loose on earth will be loosed in heaven." How do we bind an evil system? We can speak to it: "I bind this evil system [or demonic power] in Jesus' name." You will find this declaration in most circumstances to be highly effective. (Again, there may be exceptions: Jesus said there are some evil spirits so powerful that they can be bound or driven out only by combining fasting with prayer. This is one of those situations we talked about earlier where fasting may be God-ordained. We can ask the Holy Spirit to help us discern such situations, and He will do so.)

One way or another, we have the responsibility as Christians to express our opposition to Satan *somehow*. If we do not, we condone his evil deeds and enable his power to grow. I believe it was an American patriot who said, "All that is necessary for evil to triumph is for good men to do nothing." We must do *something* to fight these oppressive and destructive systems; God holds us accountable. His Spirit will reveal to us specific ways to pray against them in each situation if we seek His counsel.

How effective we are in praying for and against depends on how well we know God and His desires in our lives. I would never recommend that Christians jump into this kind of prayer without plenty of preparation and study of God's Word. It is dangerous territory— territory that is also tremendously challenging and exciting. For it is on such battlefields that we can watch God lift the world off its hinges in response to our prayers. If there is a greater thrill in this world, I don't know what it is.

Number 4: The fourth principle that will help us defeat the enemy is that we must give ourselves completely to Christ and be willing to live His life.

We must, as Paul said, "consider everything a loss compared to the surpassing greatness of knowing Christ Jesus . . . and the power of his resurrection and the fellowship of sharing his sufferings, becoming like him in his death" (Philippians 3:8, 10).

This verse of Scripture is so profound that I almost hesitate to use it in a chapter like this where we don't have the space to discuss it fully. But I cannot fail to mention it because it is vital, as we conclude our discussion of spiritual warfare, that we think and pray about whether we are prepared to live the kind of fully committed life that Jesus said we must, and that Paul in this passage challenges us to do.

It is easy to read such words and be moved by them emotionally. But do we comprehend what this kind of total commitment to God may cost us in terms of our daily existence? Too often, I'm afraid, we confuse aspiration with achievement. We think we've made the ultimate commitment when we say tearfully, "I'm Yours, Lord, heart and soul." Then, when He takes us up on it and asks us to get out of our easy chairs and do something that interferes with our own plans, we murmur and complain. "Well!" we say indignantly. "I didn't think He would ask so much! Why can't someone else do it?"

Just how far *are* we willing to go? How much of our comfort and pleasure and "security" are we willing to sacrifice, if necessary, so that others may live? How much opposition are we willing to face? We may sing that we have laid "our all on the altar"—but are we ready to lay down our possessions? our careers? our plans for a quiet, comfortable retirement? our lives? Are we willing to go where God tells us to go—even places where we might be imprisoned, tortured or killed for sharing the Gospel?

Are we, in fact, prepared to face the disapproval or ridicule of neighbors, colleagues, families or other Christians as we take a bold stand for God? When was the last time we faced the kind of persecution my friend Karl talked about—the persecution that "all who would live godly" lives must face? And if we have never faced it, are we asking ourselves why? Or are we willing to give ourselves to God only to the extent that He grants all our selfish wishes and asks nothing too hard in return?

We have to face these questions, I am convinced, if we are going to fight Satan with any real effectiveness and ask God to change His mind about what He allows Satan to do. The devil knows our strengths and weaknesses. He knows our cherished little hypocrisies. He hears our pious boasts that "we're ready to give one hundred percent to the Lord," but he also watches with glee as we grumble over the pittance we are scarcely willing to part with. He sees how little of our time we are willing to spend interceding faithfully for others and obeying Christ in taking the Gospel to our dying world. He gloats when we close our ears to the cries of the suffering Church and chortles as he notes how easily we rationalize our favorite sins by worshiping before modern Christendom's sacred idols: prosperity, success, fame and power.

Now don't misunderstand me: We don't have to be corrupted by these things. We can use wealth to promote God's work. Fame and power can be used for good instead of selfish purposes. But the sad truth is, 99 percent of the time Christians do not use the success or power God gives them in any but the most self-serving ways. They're simply not able to cope with the responsibility.

I've seen it dozens of times: A Christian will pray for "prosperity or power or fame so I can have a real impact for the Lord" (conveniently ignoring 1 Corinthians 1:27, which says that God chooses the weak and foolish things of the earth to confound the mighty). After he (or she) has poured all his time and energy into building his empire—often losing everything else in the process—he cannot bring himself to give away what he has gained. "God's portion" becomes smaller and smaller, until at last God gets little or nothing. And a potentially fruitful life ends up utterly wasted. What a sad and unnecessary victory for the devil!

The truth is, we Christians can be as reluctant as the heathen to give up any of our idols. We even imagine that God will indulge us like spoiled children, that He will perhaps let us keep our favorite idols if we clean them up a bit—that He may, in fact, even bless them if we spiritualize them enough. So we dress our idols in nice Christian costumes and invite God to give them His seal of approval. We may even pretend, as Aaron did to Moses, that they were miraculously created by God in the first place! There is apparently no limit to our self-deception.

But this is not God's will for us. He asks us to turn our backs on our idols, our halfheartedness and our selfishness so that we can finally discover what living is. The Lord has exciting plans, and He wants nothing more than to involve us in those plans. He has battles for us to fight, mountains for us to climb, exploits for us to perform, and He waits for us to do what He asks: "Follow me" (Matthew 4:19, 8:22, 9:9; Mark 2:14, 10:21; Luke 5:27, 9:23, 9:59; John 1:43, 21:19, 21:22). This brings us to our fifth and final principle for successful combat with the enemy.

Number 5: We must oppose Satan's power with the authority and love of God (Luke 10:19).

Remembering that we fight not against flesh and blood, but against Satan and his forces of evil, we must remind ourselves and each other constantly that every person on this planet is an object of God's love. Those who act the nastiest are that way because they have not known the love of God. Our task is the same one we talked about at the beginning of this chapter: to share the love of God with people who are hostages of Satan in a world under his control.

This is, to be sure, a task we cannot hope to carry out by our own power or with our own authority. God must authorize and empower us every step of the way. That is why we must be true thermostats, sensitive and responsive to the Holy Spirit's loving touch. Unless we have this kind of sensitivity, the weapons of our warfare may do more harm than good for the cause of Christ. When we blast away at the devil blindly, on our own initiative, we may find that the bullets we're using are shotgun shells that wound innocent bystanders instead of destroying our target. There are no lone rangers in God's army! We need Him—and the other members of His Body as well—to help us fight effectively.

The writer of Hebrews says it beautifully:

> Therefore, since we are surrounded by such a great
> cloud of witnesses, let us throw off everything that
> hinders and the sin that so easily entangles, and let
> us run with perseverance the race marked out for us.
> Let us fix our eyes on Jesus, the author and perfecter
> of our faith, who for the joy set before him endured
> the cross, scorning its shame, and sat down at the
> right hand of the throne of God.   Hebrews 12:1–3

That, of course, is the final and most powerful secret
of how we can manage to battle the enemy and still
represent nothing but the love of Christ. As we fix our
eyes upon Jesus and rid our lives of everything that
weighs us down, we discover that all things *are* possible
through Him. As Corrie would say if she were here
right now, this is how we become God's thermostats—
His agents of change—in a world in which the temperature is approaching the boiling point.

8
What Should We Be Asking God to Do Today?

Some years ago a woman interviewer asked me a familiar and provocative hypothetical question: If you knew you had only 24 hours to live, how would you spend your last day on earth? The question made me smile because it reminded me of the fellow who said, "If you live every day as if it were your last, someday you will be right!"

But it was a serious question and a good one—one I think we Christians should ask ourselves regularly. How would we arrange—or rearrange—our priorities if we had to squeeze everything important into just one day's time? What would we do? Where would we go? With whom would we want to spend those last precious hours?

More to the point, how would we pray? What would we ask God to do—not only for us, but for our loved ones and for the world that would go on without us? What kinds of things would we ask Him to change His mind about?

I think questions like these are a good starting point for deciding how we ought to be praying in these last days before the return of Christ. Not that we should live entirely for the moment, because that would limit our vision *and* our prayers. But there's a great deal of truth in the adage that says, "The only time we really have to spend is *now*." As the Scripture says, "Now is the day of salvation" (2 Corinthians 6:2).

But one of the beautiful things about prayer is the way it transcends the boundaries of time and distance. We may pray *now*, but the ripples caused by this day's petitions can go on and on. In a way we can barely imagine, our prayers can be immortal, reaching beyond the grave to change lives and events far into the future.

Most of us, whether we know it or not, are the beneficiaries of the prayers of people who departed this earth long before we were born. And it's safe to say that history is being changed every day, in every part of the world, as a direct result of faithful intercession by those who died without seeing their prayers answered. Like the heroes of faith in the book of Hebrews, "none of them received what had been promised. God had planned something better for us so that only together with us would they be made perfect" (Hebrews 11:39–40).

An American friend who grew up in a family of agnostics told me about his Christian grandmother, whom he never knew because she died a few months after he was born. My friend came to Christ as a young man without ever hearing the Gospel preached or knowing a single Christian, simply by reading a Bible he found at school. Some years later, after he got involved in public ministry, he received a letter from a woman who had known and prayed with his grandmother for many years before her death. "When your grandmother realized she would not live to see you," the woman wrote, "she asked me to help her pray for your salvation." Some fifteen years after the grandmother's death those prayers were answered.

In the years since then, the ripple effect has continued as other members of that family have come to know the Lord. No doubt it will continue into future generations as well, because long after my friend has left the world behind, his own prayers will continue to influence lives and events, just as his grandmother's still do and always shall.

It's a fabulous thing to consider, isn't it? There are no limits to the effects or the effectiveness of our prayers. If we want to leave our indelible mark upon the world, there is no more powerful way to do it than by getting involved in God's purposes through prayer. Our prayers can go where we cannot (although they are not a substitute for our going, if we can). There are no borders, no prison walls, no doors that are closed to us when we pray. The political, economic, military and spiritual leaders of the world may not know our names, but we can have more influence on their plans than all their closest advisers put together. While many things may be impossible from a human standpoint, in the realm of prayer there are no impossibilities. And, perhaps most exciting of all, through prayer we can reach into the future and with loving hands touch those beyond our reach, just as my friend's grandmother was able to do.

How would *you* pray if today were your last day on earth? It's a question worth answering, because it can help establish clear prayer priorities. In the process of sifting and categorizing, we can come to a better understanding of what matters most, to God as well as to us. We can then make deliberate, positive changes that will greatly improve the quality of our prayers.

So, what *should* we be asking God to do today? If I answered off the top of my head I might say, "We should ask the same kinds of things the apostles and prophets did." But that's not really a very good answer—or at least it's not a complete answer—because God loves to do new things. He is, after all, the God of creation, the God of the "new and living way" (Hebrews 10:20). Even when He chooses to do the same things again and again—like saving men's souls, healing them and calling them to ministry—He delights in finding ways to do the *same* things *differently* each time. Have you ever heard of two people who took exactly the same path to Christ? Just as no two snowflakes or sets of fingerprints are alike, no two acts of our creative God are precisely the same.

We all have our ideas about how we think God is going to work because we figure that's how He did it in Moses' time or Joshua's or Paul's or at Pentecost. But God is original. The minute we say, "We're going to give out handkerchiefs and people will be healed by touching them because that's what the apostles did," we've got a surprise coming: God will do something completely different! He doesn't want us to ritualize yesterday's experiences; He longs to reveal Himself by doing something for us *today* that He has never done before.

Often we can't accept that because we're afraid it means God can't be counted on to do *what* we want the *way* we want. We forget that while God's character and principles are unchanging, everything else about Him is "new every morning" (Lamentations 3:23) and His plan is to "make everything new" (Revelation 21:5).

This should give us a great sense of adventure about life. If we could predict everything God was going to do tomorrow, we wouldn't even need to get out of bed, would we? But the fact that He has surprises in store for us every day should be enough to make us awaken each morning with a fresh sense of wonder and an intense curiosity about what the day will hold. Where will God lead me? What will He ask me to do? For whom will He ask me to pray? And how will He answer?

You see, if we confine ourselves to asking *only* for

those things God has done in the past, or even for things we can imagine, we may actually be limiting God and losing out on some tremendous surprises and blessings. So I like to ask God to show me possibilities that have never occurred to me, things nobody has ever thought of asking Him before. I want to keep the doors open for God to do what "no eye has seen, no ear has heard, no mind has conceived" (1 Corinthians 2:9; see also Isaiah 64:4).

I suppose that's why almost all of my prayers are for *big* things, not small ones. Why should we think small? If the President of the United States invited you to the White House and promised to grant any request you made, would you use the opportunity to ask him for a new toaster—or would you begin to think in bigger terms?

We're all guilty of underestimating God. If we really knew Him as He wants us to, if we understood the potential of our prayers, we would be on our knees a hundred times a day asking Him for things that would turn the world upside-down. We would not waste our time pleading for new toasters when God says, "You may ask me for *anything* in my name, and I will do it" (John 14:14).

But we're like guests at a wedding who fight over the smallest piece of cake; we have fallen into the habit of thinking small because we think it's a sign of humility. In reality the opposite is true: If we are truly humble, we will see God's surpassing greatness and omnipotence and ask Him to raise us up to a level where His priorities become our own. Then we can begin to participate in executing His will by asking Him for things of *real* consequence.

What kinds of things am I talking about? There are a number of things I pray for—and against—in virtually all of my intercessory prayers. Part of spiritual warfare is active resistance against the hostile, so-called "natural" forces that Satan can use to destroy us or thwart God's plans for our world. Jesus often prayed against these forces. I'm thinking particularly of the time he calmed the storm on the Sea of Galilee (which I believe was another demonic attempt to kill Him) and the time He rebuked the fever from Peter's mother-in-law. (See Luke 8:24; Mark 1:31.)

I'm convinced that many events we call "natural disasters" are really satanic attacks. Storms, earthquakes, floods, forest fires—all of these could be (but are not always) the devil's attempts to kill a certain project or a person of value to God's Kingdom. We must be ready to pray against the evil forces when such disasters occur. In fact, I believe many of us have been engaged in this kind of spiritual warfare even when we haven't been conscious of what we're doing. I think, for example, of the countless mothers who pray at the bedsides of children who are burning with fever. They may not be aware of the warfare they're engaged in, but they know they are against what they see happening before their eyes, so they put up any kind of resistance they can. They pray against the fever without really understanding they are doing so, by praying for their child's recovery.

When we know about this kind of warfare, we can better choose the right weapons to fight all the so-called natural calamities Satan may utilize in his constant attempts to prevent us from doing God's will.

Once, for example, when I was preaching at a large rally in South Africa, a sudden storm arose. We were meeting in a huge tin-roofed building, so we were not insulated from the noise outside. It was the most terrible storm I'd ever experienced—trees outside were crashing to the ground, the roof was shaking, and the wind seemed to be approaching hurricane level. I realized that the roof was about to be torn off by the force of the wind. Nobody could hear anything I was saying, so I stopped and prayed, rebuking the storm. Within a few seconds the wind stopped and we went on with our meeting.

Incidents like this are commonplace for me, and they've taught me to use the weapons God has placed at our disposal. I have no hesitation about praying against the forces that might keep me from obeying God, and neither should you. The weapons of our warfare are not reserved for the giants of faith who are fighting for the nations of the earth. They have been given to all of us.

There will undoubtedly be special areas that the Holy Spirit will lead *you* to pray about, and naturally you'll want to put extra emphasis on these. God seems to give each Christian who becomes serious about intercession a few unique prayer "burdens"—a poor term for what is really a gift, but we'll use it anyway because most of us have heard it. A burden is something we become deeply motivated to pray about or act on, some part of history that God's Spirit invites us to influence through our prayers.

If we think of ourselves as thermostats, we could say that when God's touch moves us to change the temperature in a specific room, we have received a burden. It can be for an individual or a nation, a cause or a movement, a societal malaise like materialism or a localized problem like violent gang activity in our own neighborhood. We can ask God's Spirit to show us exactly what to pray for beyond the obvious big things that every Christian should be praying about today. He will *always* do it. God is delighted when we ask to become involved in what He is doing.

There is, of course, a difference between intercession and other kinds of prayer, like personal prayer about our own concerns, needs and growth, and "prayer telegrams," those urgent, instantaneous prayers in times of emergency that focus solely on an immediate threat or problem. (If I'm walking down a street in Beirut and bullets start flying past my head, I don't start praying for the people of Beijing!)

In intercession we become involved in the bigger issues of God's long-term purposes in our world, but we also focus on specific prayer for just *one* person, *one* event, *one* change that will make the difference in a situation. We join with the Body of Christ all over the world and pray in a united, dynamic way for those things that will advance God's Kingdom and defeat His enemies—and we ask Him to act in specific ways.

Using the Lord's Prayer

We can pray, in fact, as Jesus taught us in the Lord's Prayer. I believe all Christians could benefit from using the Lord's Prayer as a starting point and pattern, not just as something we memorize and recite. Jesus never intended that we do that. "Pray *like* this," He said, not, "Recite this prayer." In Ephesians 3 we can read Paul's version of the Lord's Prayer, made up of many of the same elements (Ephesians 3:14–21). I believe this is how Jesus intended His prayer to be taken. If we use His prayer as our guide for intercession (Matthew 6:9–13), we can move from the general to the specific in a very practical way.

So let's look at the Lord's Prayer as a way of organizing and focusing our prayers.

Beginning with "Our Father," we can pray for all the people we know who call Him *Father*. Sometimes I've started praying at "Our Father" and have gone on for two hours without ever getting beyond all the needs of people I know. I think of each person. I identify with him or her. I think of each church or denomination by remembering individuals within those churches and denominations, and as I pray for them we become part of each other, real family.

Then, as I pray for all those I know in the suffering Church, the world becomes smaller. I feel their pain, wrestle with their problems, and my prayers become fierce, protective, impassioned. The people of the suffering Church are my special burden, and it is on their behalf that most of my intercessions are made. I have learned of the gulags and prisons, visited clandestine churches, slept in bombed-out homes. I have seen the dead bodies, the mutilated babies, the starvation and anguish.

I can pray, "Father, You are their Father as well as mine. Show me how I can do more for these children of Yours who are suffering so terribly. Show me how to awaken the sleeping Church so *all* of us can obey Your command to care for our brothers and sisters who are so isolated, abused and tormented."

Once I begin to pray this way, my prayers become more and more specific and focused. And, I believe, more effective. All this is included when we begin to pray, "Our Father."

Then we can move on through the Lord's Prayer one phrase at a time. As we speak each phrase we can ask God, *What does this mean?* What does it mean when we pray to Him "in heaven" and say, "Hallowed be Your name"?

We say, "Your Kingdom come," and often don't understand what a profound statement and prayer that is. That includes prayer for change in everything that is imperfect, sick, maimed, sinful. We can pray on the basis that this person, this situation, this country, this tribe, this church, this government should be changed and brought into alignment with the principles of God's Kingdom—principles of justice, righteousness, soundness of mind and body and, above all, love.

It also includes prayer for such diverse Kingdom elements as Christian education, the protection of God-given liberties, the protection of the innocent, the opening of borders so Bibles and Christian missionaries can reach people in every dark corner of the world. And for the winds of change to blow in nations still controlled by Communism.

That was what our Open Doors prayer partners began to pray on December 14, 1989, just three days before the Rumanian uprising that toppled the Ceaucescu government. Our weekly prayer fax on that date read: "Pray for difficult situation of Christians in Rumania and also that in this country the winds of change may start to blow." On the same date, we asked our partners to pray "for the release of the last few prisoners being held" in the U.S.S.R.

God answered both prayers—which I'm sure were being prayed as well by countless thousands of Christians all over the world—almost overnight, and in ways that none of us could have envisioned. This should encourage us to pray with even more authority and boldness for the winds of change to blow across the whole world where people are being held hostage by evil and oppressive governments.

Then we come to "Your will be done on earth as it is in heaven." We are praying here that God's will be unopposed and unchallenged, the way it is in heaven. What a prayer and what a task! We are praying for a complete reversal of the direction this world is going. We ask, *What is Your will, Father?* and we remember what the Scriptures say—everything we talked about in chapter 3 on knowing God's will.

We know it is God's will, for example, that everyone be saved. So we can pray for all the unsaved, everyone we know. And we can pray that God will show us the best ways to reach those people so they can be saved. We can pray against the powers that would keep them from understanding the Gospel. Again, the Holy Spirit will show us how to pray as we seek His direction.

Then we remember that God's will is that we "go into all the world and preach the good news to all creation" (Mark 16:15). Thus, we can pray for every unreached tribe, every language, every city where people are not being reached with the good news of Christ. Perhaps even the people living next door!

God's will is *righteousness*. So we can remember all the unrighteousness in the world and in ourselves. There is so much unrighteousness in all of us. What do we do about our own unrighteousness? We don't wrestle with it, we don't struggle with it, we get rid of it! We *put it to death*, as Paul said (Galatians 5:16–26), so that the Spirit of God can bring fruitfulness to our lives. We *put away* all the works of the flesh mentioned in that passage, everything from adultery to witchcraft to envy, and we *put on* the garments of the Spirit: goodness, faith, patience, moderation, joy, peace, gentleness, meekness and above all love, which binds everything together in perfect harmony.

Then, as we pray further about righteousness and unrighteousness, we can think about the unrighteous-

175

ness of war, hatred, crime, violence, stealing, immorality, excesses of all kinds. It pours a stream of compassion into our hearts as we pray in these areas.

As you pray for God's will for the nations, your thinking enlarges as the world grows smaller. And perhaps not the first or the second time you pray, but the fifth and the tenth, you begin to see the nations as you have never seen them before. You may even read and study about specific places as God brings them to mind. Your interest and faith will increase as you begin to understand something about people you never knew existed. You may find out that Timbuktu is a real place—that it's the largest city in the nation of Mali, in Africa. Thousands of people there have never seen the Bible, never heard the Gospel. You begin to pray for them, and for the missionaries and churches reaching out to them.

This leads you to become interested in many other remote areas of the world, and you discover there are more than three thousand languages that do not have the Bible. How can they know or *do* the will of God—which is what you've been praying for in the Lord's Prayer—if they don't have the Bible? As you think about this you begin to pray for Bible translators. You discover who some of them are so you can pray for them as individuals and as organizations. You start giving your money to support them. Then maybe one day while you're praying, God puts the thought into your head that you're pretty good with languages. Why couldn't you join an organization like Wycliffe that translates the Bible into new languages?

You see what can happen as you pray, "Your will be done"!

As you pray for God's will, you'll also find that your prayers begin to become much more personal. Instead of praying vaguely and generally for "laborers for the harvest," pretty soon you'll find yourself praying, "God, use *me* to reach my family, my neighbors and my city."

Praying for God's will is a risky matter. If we are really seeking His will, we will end up committing ourselves to joining those on the firing line and making ourselves targets for the enemy. If we ask God to make us prophets we will become unpopular. We will be laughed at, reviled and persecuted for righteousness' sake, because not a single prophet in the Bible was ever popular or accepted by the people of his community. But all the prophets made history—not because they were great, but because they submitted their cause to an almighty God and His authority became theirs.

There will be times, of course, when you look at a situation and say, "Lord, that *cannot* be Your will! And if it is, then I want You to change Your mind about it." You toss the ball back to God. Your intercessions become desperate and intense. And God's Spirit enters into your prayers, prompting you to pray in ways you have never prayed before.

You may be praying for missionaries and suddenly think, "Why are there no missionaries going out from *my* church? Why hasn't God called anyone in our fellowship [or Bible study] to serve on the mission field?"

So you begin to pray, "Father, I want You to change Your mind about that. I want You to call *us*." That is praying for God's will to be done.

You know, in my fellowship in Holland, one hundred percent of the young people have gone onto the mission field. Not one has stayed home. I'm the worst missionary in the bunch from their point of view because, as they say, "Andrew always comes back!" (The others stay away from home five years or more at a stretch. They're *real* missionaries.) But we prayed that God would call *us*, and He has! The only people in our fellowship who have not gone onto the mission field are those too old or too sick to go. They have a big job to do, however: They pray, give, train others and do everything in their power to support those who are going and have already gone to the field.

As I suggested in chapter 6, that's what the local church is supposed to be: a recruiting station, a basic training camp, a support and supply conduit for those called to the front. It was *never* intended to become a center for entertainment, social activity, self-promotion or empire-building.

That, unfortunately, is what the church is in many places today. Some of our biggest Christian churches have absolutely zero impact on their communities and the world because they are nothing more than luxurious showcases for people who want to "feel good about themselves" and impress each other with the way God has "blessed" them, instead of doing what God has commanded them to do. They are places where Christians can devote themselves to the pursuit of happiness instead of to the pursuit of God's Kingdom. They import an endless succession of celebrities and entertainers who feed people's desire for distraction and drama, and in the process anesthetize them so they no longer feel the pain in the Body of Christ.

I have been in many of these churches. I have preached in them. And I am appalled and saddened by what I see: a herd of Christians so busy tapping their feet to the music, so entranced by the showcase of talent up on stage, and pastors so consumed with the task of counting new members (and building ever bigger and more elaborate edifices to house and entertain them on Sunday) that hardly anyone hears the cries of those who are suffering and dying all over the globe—or even in the few square miles surrounding their church building. And when someone like Brother Andrew tries to challenge them with the truth, they refuse to accept it because that would mean getting up and leaving the beautiful cocoon they have built to protect and comfort themselves. No wonder we are losing the battle for men's souls!

Now, are you beginning to see what happens when we get serious about praying, "Your will be done"? As we look at all the things we *know* to be God's will and we begin to pray for them to happen—as thermostats we click on and start doing what we were designed to do—we cause *change*.

Too many Christians say, "Oh, I want the Lord's will to be done. But what can one person's prayers really accomplish in terms of the whole world?" Too many Christians use that as an excuse not to pray. But if only one person knows God, that person's light shines all the more brightly in the dark. If only one person in five billion really understands and communicates with God, the five billion can never say He doesn't exist, because one gram of experience weighs more than ten tons of argument.

Once we believers have finished praying for everything that comes under the heading of "Your will be done," we can begin to pray, "Give us today our daily bread"—which is a prayer not just for my own bread, but for that of the whole Body that needs nourishment and strengthening. We can pray for the practical and personal needs of our families, our friends, our co-workers—all who have spiritual and physical and emotional needs.

We can pray for those suffering from famines and epidemics or from disasters like floods and earthquakes in all parts of the world. We can pray for healing, deliverance, provision, *whatever is essential to enable people to do the work God has called them to do.*

"Give us this day" prayers are not "gimme" prayers or "bless me" prayers. We should never get into a selfish habit of asking God to "bless me"; we should be praying for *others* to be blessed, and as our lives begin to count for others, that will be *our* blessing. If I insist upon asking for selfish blessings, God may give them to me. Sometimes the only way we'll learn our lesson is to experience the consequences of our own selfishness.

"O.K.," God may say, "you can have your bag of candy. If you want to get sick, get sick. Maybe you'll learn." Many of us never learn, unfortunately, and we get stuck in the habit of asking for candy because it tastes good and makes us happy for a little while, even though in the long run it only rots our teeth and makes us fat and lazy. God shakes His head and says, "If that's what you want, I won't say no, but you'll have to pay the price."

The price of selfish prayer is almost always a terrible one, for us and for the lives we should be influencing for God. We become unfruitful, purposeless, ineffective, and our lives cease to have any meaning at all in terms of God's plans and purposes.

And this leads us to pray, "Forgive us our debts, as we also have forgiven our debtors." We must forgive if we want to be forgiven. It's a two-way street. Most of us don't take these words of Christ seriously enough.

I was visiting with a good friend of mine, a woman in the Middle East who is both a Christian and with the P.L.O. A shocking combination in some people's eyes, but I find Christians sometimes in the strangest places! Even more surprising, in the middle of our visit this woman said to me, "Andrew, Christianity has become for me a daily commitment. My greatest struggle is to forgive my enemies. How can I forgive those who want to kill me and my brothers and sisters, and who would deny me my homeland? But I *must* forgive. I get on my face before God and I sweat over this. I want to say, *'God, I forgive my enemies.'* I picture them, I see what they are doing every day. I see the dead bodies, the suffer-

181

ing, the blood. I try to forgive, but I cannot. So I pray, *'God, You must help me forgive, because I cannot!'* "

I tell you, I was deeply impressed with that woman, and I know God is much more impressed with her wrestling prayers than He is with all the silly, foolish ones that attempt to wipe the slate clean with one easy swipe: "God bless all our friends and enemies, Amen!" That woman is struggling with issues the magnitude of which most of us have never even imagined. She's serious about forgiveness, which I believe is a sign of great maturity.

We often seem to think we can brush aside the forgiveness part of the Lord's Prayer. "Well, sure, I forgive my enemies," we say, carefully adjusting our halos. But then we go on our way nursing our petty grudges and clinging to memories of insults and offenses that happened years ago. We don't struggle over our lack of forgiveness because we think we're *entitled*—and we don't see the harm in it. We don't fall on our faces and say, "God, I *will* forgive—help my unforgiveness!" We shrug it off by saying, "I'm perfectly willing to forgive those who have hurt me—when they come to me and beg me." Or we take the attitude of a fellow named Heinrich Heine, who said back in the early 1800s, "One should forgive one's enemies, but not before they are hanged."

Sure, we can laugh, because we're all in the same boat. We all have things to forgive that we don't want to forgive, just as we fail to ask forgiveness because we don't want to admit we've done anything wrong. We would rather rationalize our sin than admit it and have to change. But we want to see others punished, even if we have to do the punishing ourselves.

Until we begin to get serious about letting go of our bitterness and anger, however, the way that woman in the P.L.O. did, our prayer lives will be stuck in the mud of unforgiveness and we won't see God doing all that He wants to do in and through us.

Now we reach the part of the Lord's Prayer that says, "Lead us not into temptation, but deliver us from the evil one." This is where we ask God to equip us for battle and guard us and the whole Body of Christ against temptation. Again, we must make this more than a selfish prayer, because if we don't pray for one another in this regard, we leave our brothers and sisters open to attack.

I often wonder whether many of the prominent Christians whose lives and ministries have been destroyed by their moral and spiritual failure during the past few years might not have been kept from such failure if those in the Church had been praying for them as they should. Not that these prominent men and women are not personally responsible for their choices; we're all responsible, and we will be held accountable by God. It's just that we must recognize that when one member of the Body fails, we all fail, and we are responsible for each other. We must not point our fingers and say, "How *could* they?" We must examine ourselves and say, "How could *we?*" and, "What could I have done to prevent this?"

We are that intimately connected, you see. When I see my brother fall, I must remember that I *am* my brother's keeper. It is my responsibility to pray, to support, to do everything possible to keep him from falling. And if he *does* fall—regardless of how or why—it is also my responsibility to help restore him as a functioning member of the Body. We cannot afford to do otherwise.

This is also where we combat satanic schemes and systems, as we discussed in the last chapter. We pray against such evils as drug trafficking and addiction, rampant corruption and sin in every area from government to business to the arts, international terrorism, crime, the rise of false religions and the occult, and the tyranny of atheistic systems like Communism, fascism and a hundred other "isms" from which the world needs to be delivered. (In spite of the changes we've seen in Eastern Europe and the Soviet Union, Communism is still responsible for more suffering on a worldwide scale than any other system or entity, so I call upon all Christians to continue to attack one of Satan's primary strongholds by praying against Communism.)

It is in this area of intercession that we must also learn to pray that God will remove from our lives all that keeps us superficial in our relationship with Him. Superficiality is the greatest peril in the Christian life. Satan wants nothing more than to keep us superficial. I'm terribly serious about this, not only in my own life, but in that of the Church at large. Not a single prophet I know of has warned us adequately about this terrible danger.

In the last half of the twentieth century the Church has become more superficial than I ever imagined possible. We say we want to see God, we want to be used, we want to see the miracles the apostles saw, we want to have "the deeper life." But our lives and our personal relationships with God are so shallow that most Christians never get close to that kind of experience. We want to *look* and *sound* like the Christians we read about in the Bible, but because we are not prepared to pray, live and sacrifice as they did, we accept substitutes for a genuine Christian experience that satisfy our need for drama and excitement and leave us powerless, weak and ineffectual.

We shout *hallelujah* and raise our hands because that's what believers did at Pentecost, and we may exhibit "gifts of the Spirit" that we've manufactured ourselves because we have no idea what the *real* gifts of the Spirit are like.

We may even accept prophecies that do not come from God because we don't really know God's voice, and as a result we have no way of telling when a false prophet speaks in His place. In fact, I am convinced that in many churches today the devil himself could appear and shout, "Thus saith the Lord . . ." and we would not challenge him because many of us don't know the difference between his voice and God's. As a result the Church is easily led astray by false prophets and charlatans. What a tragedy!

We may little know what it's like when the power of the Holy Spirit *actually* comes down on His people the way He did at Pentecost, and as He has in all the great

185

revivals in history. And we're not really prepared to have our lives turned upside-down as they would be if we *did* experience that kind of visitation. Most of us are not ready to have our comfortable, secure existences shattered forever.

When I preach in large churches in Europe and America I sometimes ask, as I begin my message, "If God had died yesterday, would anybody here have noticed?" It shocks everyone, and that's what I want. Then I go on to suggest that they have arranged their lives in such a way that they don't really *need* or *want* a living God who disturbs the status quo—a God intimately involved on a moment-to-moment basis in every decision and activity of their lives.

Everything is decided and planned in advance, so it would only be an inconvenience if they asked Him to get involved on Sunday morning. After all, they came to church already knowing with whom they were going to sit, how much they were going to put into the collection plate and where they would go as soon as the service ended (and it had better end on schedule, because they wouldn't want to arrive late!).

The pastor and his staff probably already decided the songs they would sing, the prayers they would pray, the Scriptures they would read, the sermon that would be preached and even the announcements they were going to make. It's all printed right there in the bulletin! If there's a time set aside for the congregation to request prayer or to offer thanksgiving, it is limited to a strict five- or ten-minute period.

Then I like to ask, "When was the last time you heard a pastor get into a pulpit and say, 'God hasn't given me a message today, so we're going to sing a song and pray together and go home'?" As pastors we are often more concerned with our reputations and the expectations of the congregation than we are about hearing from God. And we can always pull out one of our books of sermon topics and put together a nice sermon if God doesn't give us one. Or we can preach a message we've preached before. I have done it myself more times than I like to admit. It's too easy. And it's made easier by the fact that most congregations are so superficial in their walks with God that they won't know the difference between a message breathed by God and one that comes out of a book of stale sermons.

That is a great pity. We're in this fix together! We must expect more of each other and of God.

When I have finished saying all this to the congregation, I ask them again: "If God had died yesterday, would you have noticed?" It shakes them up—I hope. They may not like it, but that doesn't concern me. What concerns me is that believers wake up and rediscover who God is and what He is doing today. And we must not accept lukewarmness in our own hearts. We must get ourselves by the scruffs of our own necks and *do* something instead of sitting week after week in our churches waiting to be entertained! We must become thermostats instead of thermometers, causing *change* in response to the Holy Spirit's touch. But if we never get close enough to Him to experience His touch, and if we never hear His voice, how can we?

"Deliver us from the evil one" must therefore include our prayer that God will deliver us from shallow Christianity—the lifeless, superficial lifestyle that pays lip service to everything Jesus did for us on the cross, and leaves God outside the front door where we won't have to bother with Him unless we have an urgent problem. We need to be delivered from our desire to claim the blessings God has given to the Church through the ages without paying the price they paid.

I'm not talking about salvation here—for that, of course, there is no price to be paid, because Jesus paid it all. But there *is* a price to be paid for the privileges God gives only to those who know and love Him. We cannot have such privileges or blessings without cost. How much are we willing to pay? What are we willing to give up so God can use us?

Are we willing to become a proletarian people? Are we willing to give up our middle-class and upper-class lifestyles? We don't *have* to have a prestigious job, our kids don't *have* to go to the "best" colleges, we don't *have* to have a second car or a second home or a second television at the cost of everything that's important, including our relationship with God. Jesus said, "The man who loves his life will lose it, while the man who hates his life in this world will keep it for eternal life" (John 12:25). Do we believe Him? Are we willing to *live* it?

Jesus also said, as we quoted earlier,

"As the Father has loved me, so have I loved you. Now remain in my love. If you obey my commands, you will remain in my love, just as I have obeyed my Father's commands and remain in his love. I have told you this so that my joy may be in you and that your joy may be complete. My command is this: Love each other as I have loved you. Greater love has no one than this, that one lay down his life for his friends. You are my friends if you do what I command. . . . You did not choose me, but I chose you to go and bear fruit—fruit that will last. Then the Father will give you whatever you ask in my name. This is my command: Love each other."

John 15:9–14, 16–17

When we fully comprehend what this means in terms of the courageous decisions we must make every day of our lives, we will be elevated to that level at which we can become true intercessors—which is a level passive or superficial Christians can never understand. They may call us "out-of-touch," "super-spiritual" or "fanatical," not realizing we are the only ones who are in touch with reality, because we're the only ones in a position to tackle causes instead of having to deal with symptoms like the rest of the world. We're the ones who can *cause change* instead of merely *reacting* to it.

When we reach this level, our lives become really exciting! We begin to live in the supernatural realm, where God and His purposes are a reality greater than any other and His desires have become our own. Our minds and spirits unite with His, and we live, move and have our beings in Him.

It is here that we come full-circle from the point where

we began to talk about changing God's mind. Here we pray the final words of Jesus' prayer, "For Yours is the Kingdom and the power and the glory forever." When we know His will for His Kingdom, we will be able to ask God to change His mind about allowing anything short of that to continue.

Paul's expanded prayer in Ephesians ends,

> Now to him who is able to do immeasurably more than all we ask or imagine, according to his power that is at work within us, to him be glory in the church and in Christ Jesus throughout all generations, for ever and ever! Amen.   Ephesians 3:20–21

How do we begin to realize what it means to be children of the living God who is not only able but willing to do "immeasurably more than all we ask or imagine"? How do we respond when God says, "Ask of me, and I will make the nations your inheritance, the ends of the earth your possession" (Psalm 2:8)?

Yes, we must *ask* for the nations and for the ends of the earth. God will give them to us! The unsaved world is waiting for us to ask. Our oppressed brothers and sisters in the suffering Church are waiting for us to ask. Above all, God is waiting for us to ask. "This is a people plundered and looted," God reminds us, "all of them trapped in pits or hidden away in prisons . . . with no one to rescue them . . . no one to say, 'Send them back.' Which of you will listen to this or pay close attention in time to come?" (Isaiah 42:22–23).

Which of us will listen? Will *you*? Will you be that one who will throw off fatalism, step forward to stand in the gap, to rescue the nations and claim the inheritance God has promised? Will you be that one willing to risk *everything* for the sake of God's Kingdom, power and glory?

If you will, God says, "I will answer you . . . I will help you . . . to restore the land and to reassign its desolate inheritances, to say to the captives, 'Come out,' and to those in darkness, 'Be free!' " (Isaiah 49:8–9).

That is our holy calling and commission, and that is also the greatest adventure life offers. Let's go for it—together!

In 1955, God spoke to the heart of a young Dutch missionary with the words, "Awake, and strengthen what remains and is on the point of death" (Revelation 3:2). From that day, **Brother Andrew** believed that no doors could be closed to the Gospel. In his now-famous little blue Volkswagen, he began making trips to nearly every country in the Communist bloc, and then to Russia itself. He personally delivered Bibles across "closed" borders and encouraged the persecuted believers who remained behind the Iron Curtain. Then came trips behind the Bamboo Curtain, and into Africa, Cuba, Central and South America and the Middle East.

God's Smuggler, the account of Andrew's early years, was published in 1967, selling over ten million copies in 27 languages and becoming a Christian classic.

In the years since the publication of that book, some three hundred co-workers have joined with Andrew to further extend his ministry. Today, Open Doors with Brother Andrew coordinates major projects to strengthen and equip the persecuted church on the front lines in 45 countries worldwide.

To learn more about the ministry of Open Doors and to receive a complimentary six-month subscription to their monthly newsletter, *Newsbrief*, please contact them at:

Open Doors USA	Open Doors Canada
P.O. Box 27001	P.O. Box 597
Santa Ana, CA 92799	Streetsville, ON L5M 2C1
949-752-6600	905-821-6303
usa@opendoors.org	opendoorsca@compuserve.com

Susan Devore Williams is the award-winning author of several nonfiction books and a popular novel, *Sunset Coast*. Her articles have appeared in a variety of publications, including *Guideposts* and *Reader's Digest*. She and her husband live in the rural Midwest.